Good Housekeeping FAVORITE RECIPES

APPETIZERS!

From top clockwise: Crab-Stuffed Mushrooms, Alaskan Salmon Spread, Spicy Dallas Cheese Straws

Good Housekeeping FAVORITE RECIPES

APPETIZERS!

The Editors of Good Housekeeping

HEARST BOOKS
A DIVISION OF STERLING PUBLISHING CO., INC.
NEW YORK

Ellen Levine **Editor in Chief**

Susan Westmoreland **Food Director**

Susan Deborah **Associate Food**
Goldsmith **Director**

Delia Hammock **Nutrition Director**

Sharon Franke **Food Appliances**
Director

Richard Eisenberg **Special Projects**
Director

Marilu Lopez **Design Director**

Book Design by Renato Stanisic

Photography Credits
Sang An: Page 19
James Baigrie: Pages 20, 149
Beatriz Da Costa: Pages 124–125
Brian Hagiwara: Pages 6, 8, 14–15, 25,
89, 170, 200–201, 206
Rita Maas: Pages 91, 120, 161, 166, 181
Steven Mark Needham: Page 117
Alan Richardson: Pages 64, 80, 132,
209, 213, 229
Ann Stratton: Pages 2, 12, 51, 74–75, 77, 98,
129, 137, 144, 158, 184, 214, 222–223
Mark Thomas: Pages 29, 58, 187, 203

Library of Congress
Cataloging-in-Publication Data

Appetizers : favorite recipes / the editors
of Good housekeeping.
p. cm.
Includes index.
ISBN 1-58816-515-9
1. Appetizers. I. Good housekeeping
(New York, N.Y.)
TX740.A725 2006
641.8'12--dc22

2005021991

Published by Hearst Books
A Division of Sterling Publishing Co., Inc.
387 Park Avenue South, New York, NY 10016

Good Housekeeping and Hearst Books
are trademarks owned by
Hearst Communications, Inc.

The Good Housekeeping Cookbook Seal
guarantees that the recipes in this cookbook
meet the strict standards of the Good
Housekeeping Institute, a source of reliable
information and a consumer advocate since
1900. Every recipe has been triple-tested
for ease, reliability, and great taste.

www.goodhousekeeping.com

For information about custom editions, special
sales, premium and corporate purchases, please
contact Sterling Special Sales Department at
800-805-5489 or specialsales@sterlingpub.com.

Distributed in Canada by Sterling Publishing
c/o Canadian Manda Group, 165 Dufferin Street
Toronto, Ontario, Canada M6K 3H6

Distributed in Australia by Capricorn Link
(Australia) Pty. Ltd.
P.O. Box 704, Windsor, NSW 2756 Australia

Manufactured in China

Sterling ISBN 13: 978-1-58816-515-2
ISBN 10: 1-58816-515-9

CONTENTS

Lemony White-Bean Bruchetta

FOREWORD

As someone who is consistently drawn to the appetizer sections of restaurant menus, I'm excited to add Appetizers! to this series of *Good Housekeeping* Favorites cookbooks. Why? Appetizers, or apps as we lovingly refer to them, are fun food. They aren't a necessary part of a meal but just their appearance on a coffee table can create a festive party mood. Whether you are hosting an all out hors d'oeuvres cocktail party, looking for something to keep your guests mingling while you put finishing touches on the main dish, or just want a great snack, Appetizers! offers a wide variety of delicious choices.

And the good news about many of the appetizers in this book—some take less than 10 minutes to put together, and many others can be done ahead so you'll have time to focus on your guests.

The recipes are a collection of our favorites from across the country and around the globe, so whether you are in the mood for Buffalo wings, guacamole or sushi, you'll find a recipe to please. Entertaining children? Try the Peanut-Ginger Dip—it just might get the children in your life to eat more veggies. As always the recipes have all been triple-tested to ensure great taste and easy prep so have a party and enjoy—the apps are sure to be a hit!

Artichoke Dip

APPETIZERS

Appetizers serve two important roles: they whet one's appetite and set the tone for the meal that follows. A stylish sit-down dinner calls for an elegant first course that looks terrific on your best china. Mini Crab Cakes (page 121) would be an excellent choice for a menu featuring a main course of meat. A casual backyard barbecue requires a different approach. Heaping bowls of fuss-free dips and chips are always popular with both guests and cooks at this kind of informal gathering. At a cocktail party, the hors d'oeuvres are the meal, so you'll want to offer a wide selection. This is the time to prepare bite-size savory pastries, such as Curried Cheddar Puffs (page 153) and finger food, such as Roasted Prosciutto–Wrapped Asparagus (page 133). Some of our favorite appetizers are simple dips, breads, and nibbles, meant to be served without ceremony to soothe simple hunger pains.

It is important to balance the appetizers you serve with the rest of the menu. When choosing the first course for a dinner, avoid repeating the flavors of the main course. For a party where lots of hors d'oeuvres will be served, the selection should reflect a variety of flavors, textures, shapes, and temperatures to keep guests tempted. Consider the colors of the food, too. Appetizers that are baked until golden brown are delicious, but they need to be garnished creatively and served alongside more colorful offerings. A garnish doesn't have to be fancy, however. It can be as simple as a small cluster of green grapes or a few little apples or pears. Or take a cue from the recipe. A few clusters of fresh red and green chiles can look dramatic on a platter of Mexican-inspired goodies.

The recipes offered in this book reflect cuisines from all over the globe, including Vietnam, Indonesia, China, France, Italy, Mexico, Greece, and Spain. While it can be fun to feature the food of a specific region when serving a variety of appetizers, it isn't necessary to stay within the culinary borders of one country or area. Simply avoid serving appetizers that are too similar to the other dishes on the menu. Once you've chosen something such as Spicy Dallas Cheese Straws (page 99), for example, steer clear of other recipes that contain Cheddar cheese and puff pastry.

The last chapter in the book is "Sweet Finales," where you'll be sure to find a couple of luscious bite-size desserts to serve at a party. These are the grand finale at an hors d'oeuvre party. Praline Brownies can almost always elicit a swoon—and a request for the recipe.

How to Manage the Menu

- Prepare as many appetizers in advance as possible. Among the best candidates are marinated olives and vegetables, dips, spreads, baked savory pastries, pâtés, and terrines.
- Don't select too many appetizers that demand last-minute attention. Arrange finished hors d'oeuvres in jelly-roll pans, then cover and refrigerate. If you are running short of space, invert a large roasting pan over a large platter and place a second platter on top.
- For appetizers that require last-minute assembling, prepare and chill the separate components until serving time.
- Plan on only one or two hot appetizers. Unless you have more than one oven, it's too difficult to juggle reheating more than a few items. Too many hot hors d'oeuvres also means more time spent in the kitchen than with your guests.
- Be sure to serve some appetizers, like nuts, dips, spreads, and pâtés, that require no more work than simply setting them out and checking occasionally for replenishment. A menu comprised of passed hors d'oeuvres is only good if you have lots of help.
- Consider the amount of available refrigerator space when planning your menu. To save room, store dips, spreads, and marinated olives in zip-tight plastic bags.
- Tea sandwiches and other miniature sandwiches make excellent appetizers, and there's quite a selection to choose from (pages 192 to 196). Make the sandwiches ahead and arrange them in jelly-roll pans. Separate the layers with damp paper towels and cover securely with plastic wrap to keep them from drying out.

• How much should you serve? Figure on ten to twelve small appetizers per person if no meal follows. Otherwise, allow five or six pieces per guest.

Do-Ahead Strategies

• Prepare vegetables for crudités up to one day ahead. Wrap them in damp paper towels, store in zip-tight plastic bags, and refrigerate. Asparagus, broccoli, green beans, and cauliflower are best when lightly cooked (blanched). Trim and cut the vegetables into the desired size or shape (flowerets, spears, or sticks) and boil in lightly salted water just until tender-crisp (usually no longer than two minutes). Drain in a colander, rinse well with cold running water, and pat dry with paper towels. Store as directed.
• Most pâtés and terrines are best if made one or two days ahead. Wrap them tightly in foil and refrigerate. Meat pâtés freeze well for up to two months when double-wrapped in foil. Defrost overnight in the refrigerator.
• Freeze pastry appetizers, such as Empanaditas (page 150), raw or baked, for up to one month. Layer the pastries in shallow baking pans (disposable aluminum foil pans work well), separating the layers with waxed paper. Wrap each pan tightly with a double layer of foil. To serve, unwrap the pastries and arrange them on cookie sheets. Reheat the baked pastries in a 350°F oven for about ten minutes before serving. Or bake the raw pastries straight from the freezer as the recipe directs, allowing a little additional baking time.

Serving with Style

• Appetizers should be easy to handle, easy to eat, and take no more than a couple of bites to finish. Set out bowls for olive pits, toothpicks, and kabob skewers—and don't forget the cocktail napkins.
• Arrange cut-up vegetables on a tray or in a large basket lined with plastic wrap and covered with a bed of curly endive, green or purple kale, or other leafy salad greens.
• For a change of pace, serve dips and spreads in hollowed-out loaves of bread, squash, or cabbage.
• For a buffet-style party, use flat dishes that hold a generous quantity of food. To create the most dramatic presentation, add height by placing

Homemade Sushi

some platters on inverted baking dishes or on boxes covered with napkins that are color-coordinated with the tablecloth.

- Store-bought crackers come in a wide assortment of shapes and flavors. Plain and mildly seasoned crackers, such as sesame or poppy, are the most versatile and can accompany a variety of savory spreads and pâtés. Herb- or garlic-flavored crackers compete with, rather than complement, aromatic spreads or strong-flavored cheeses. When serving thinly sliced bread (French baguettes work well with many dishes), store in zip-tight plastic bags until the last minute to keep the bread fresh.

- Homemade toasts, from pita bread wedges or thinly sliced baguettes, are a welcome alternative to crackers and they're easy to make. Brush the bread with olive oil or melted butter and bake in a preheated 350°F oven until lightly browned, about ten minutes. Store at room temperature in an airtight container.

- For the most flavor, remove cold appetizers from the refrigerator about thirty minutes before serving, but don't let them stand at room temperature for longer than two hours.

- The microwave is ideal for reheating non-pastry appetizers, such as Chicken and Beef Saté (page 171). Appetizer pastries are best reheated in a conventional oven—microwaving makes them soggy.

DIPS & SPREADS

Clockwise from Top: Green Herb Sauce, Cucumber Salsa, Roasted Red Pepper Puree, Cajun Rémoulade Sauce

Guacamole

Whether it's the Super Bowl or summer, this popular Mexican specialty is a *must*. Use as a dip for tortilla chips, dollop onto nachos, or serve alongside sizzling steak, burgers, or grilled chicken.

PREP: 15 MINUTES MAKES ABOUT 3 CUPS

2 ripe medium avocados, halved, pitted, and peeled
2 ripe medium tomatoes, coarsely chopped
1 jalapeño chile, seeded and minced

1 cup loosely packed fresh cilantro leaves, chopped
1 tablespoon fresh lime juice
1/2 teaspoon salt

Place avacado flesh in medium bowl and mash avocados. Add tomatoes, jalapeño, cilantro, lime juice, and salt; stir gently to combine. If not serving right away, press plastic wrap onto surface and refrigerate up to 4 hours. Stir before serving.

Each 1/4 cup: About 55 calories, 1g protein, 3g carbohydrate, 5g total fat (1g saturated), 2g fiber, 0mg cholesterol, 105mg sodium.

Roasted Red Pepper and Walnut Dip

A luscious party dip with a Middle Eastern accent.

PREP: 30 MINUTES PLUS COOLING BROIL: 8 MINUTES
MAKES ABOUT 2 CUPS

4 medium red bell peppers
$1/2$ cup walnuts
$1/2$ teaspoon ground cumin
2 slices firm white bread, torn into pieces
2 tablespoons raspberry or balsamic vinegar

1 tablespoon olive oil
$1/2$ teaspoon salt
$1/8$ teaspoon ground red pepper (cayenne)
toasted pita bread triangles

1. Preheat broiler. Line broiling pan with foil. Cut each red pepper lengthwise in half; remove and discard stems and seeds. Arrange peppers, cut side down, in prepared pan. Place pan in broiler, 5 to 6 inches from heat source. Broil peppers, without turning, until skin is charred and blistered, 8 to 10 minutes. Wrap peppers in foil and allow to steam at room temperature 15 minutes or until cool enough to handle.

2. Meanwhile, turn oven control to 350°F. Spread walnuts in metal baking pan and bake 8 to 10 minutes, until toasted. In 8-inch skillet, toast cumin over low heat until fragrant, 1 to 2 minutes. Remove from heat.

3. Remove peppers from foil. Peel skin and discard. Cut peppers into large pieces.

4. In food processor with knife blade attached, process walnuts until ground. Add roasted peppers, bread, vinegar, olive oil, cumin, salt, and ground red pepper; puree until smooth. Transfer to serving bowl. Cover and refrigerate up to 4 hours. Remove from refrigerator 30 minutes before serving. Serve with toasted pita triangles.

Each tablespoon: About 25 calories, 0g protein, 2g carbohydrate, 2g total fat (0g saturated), 1g fiber, 0mg cholesterol, 40mg sodium.

Red Pepper and Dried Tomato Dip

PREP: 30 MINUTES PLUS COOLING   BROIL: 8 MINUTES
MAKES ABOUT 1 1/2 CUPS

2 large red peppers
8 oil-packed dried tomatoes, drained
2 tablespoons capers, drained
2 teaspoons fresh lemon juice
1 small garlic clove, crushed with
   garlic press
1/2 teaspoon salt

1/4 teaspoon coarsely ground black
   pepper
2 tablespoons extravirgin olive oil
1/4 cup loosely packed fresh parsley
   leaves
toasted pita bread wedges
assorted vegetables

1. Preheat broiler. Line broiling pan with foil. Cut each red pepper lengthwise in half; remove and discard stems and seeds. Arrange peppers, cut side down, in prepared pan. Place pan in broiler, 5 to 6 inches from source of heat. Broil peppers, without turning, until skin is charred and blistered, 8 to 10 minutes. Wrap peppers in foil and allow to steam at room temperature for 15 minutes or until cool enough to handle.

2. Remove peppers from foil. Peel off skin and discard. Cut peppers into large pieces.

3. In food processor with knife blade attached, combine peppers, dried tomatoes, capers, lemon juice, garlic, salt, and black pepper; pulse until finely chopped. With processor running, gradually add oil through feed tube, processing until mixture is smooth. Add parsley; pulse to blend. Transfer to serving bowl. If not serving right away, cover and refrigerate up to 2 days. Serve with pita bread wedges and assorted vegetables.

Each tablespoon: About 15 calories, 0g protein, 1g carbohydrate, 1g total fat (0g saturated), 0g fiber, 0mg cholesterol, 75mg sodium.

Red Pepper and Dried Tomato Dip

Dried Tomato Dip

Dried Tomato Dip

All the ingredients for this easy dip get pulsed in the food processor. Serve with cut-up vegetables and/or sturdy potato chips.

PREP: 15 MINUTES   MAKES ABOUT 2 CUPS

1 package (8 ounces) Neufchâtel
1/2 cup reduced-fat sour cream
1/2 cup light mayonnaise
1 teaspoon white wine vinegar
3/4 teaspoon coarsely ground black
  pepper
1/2 teaspoon salt

1/8 teaspoon ground red pepper
  (cayenne)
1/4 cup oil-packed dried tomatoes,
  drained
1/2 cup loosely packed fresh basil
  leaves

1. In food processor with knife blade attached, combine Neufchâtel, sour cream, mayonnaise, vinegar, black pepper, salt, and ground red pepper; puree until smooth.

2. Add dried tomatoes; pulse just until tomatoes are coarsely chopped. Add basil; pulse just until coarsely chopped. Transfer to serving bowl. If not serving right away, cover and refrigerate up to 4 days.

Each tablespoon: About 40 calories, 1g protein, 1g carbohydrate, 4g total fat (2g saturated), 0g fiber, 8mg cholesterol, 90mg sodium.

Creamy Veggie Dip

Our vegetable-studded dip is best if refrigerated for at least four hours so the flavors have a chance to develop. Serve with crudités, bagel chips, or breadsticks.

Prep: 25 minutes   Makes about 4 cups

1 medium carrot, peeled and cut into 2-inch pieces
5 medium radishes
1/2 red pepper, cut into quarters
1 small stalk celery, cut into 2-inch pieces
2 green onions, cut into 2-inch pieces
1 package (3 ounces) cream cheese, softened
1/2 cup light mayonnaise
1 container (16 ounces) reduced-fat sour cream
1 1/2 teaspoons freshly grated lemon peel
1/2 teaspoon salt
1/2 teaspoon ground black pepper

1. In food processor with knife blade attached, combine carrot, radishes, red pepper, celery, and green onions; process until finely chopped. Transfer vegetables to medium bowl.

2. In food processor with knife blade attached, process cream cheese and mayonnaise until smooth. Add to vegetables in bowl. Add sour cream, lemon peel, salt, and pepper; stir until well blended. Cover and refrigerate at least 4 hours or up to 2 days. Stir before serving.

Each tablespoon: About 20 calories, 0g protein, 1g carbohydrate, 2g total fat (1g saturated), 0g fiber, 5mg cholesterol, 40mg sodium.

Toasted Sesame Dip

A new twist on the old-fashioned, classic relish tray. The unusual mixture of kosher salt and toasted white and black sesame seeds makes a delicious dip for radishes, celery, and carrot sticks—and so simple! If you're having trouble finding black sesame seeds, use one-half cup toasted white sesame seeds plus one tablespoon poppy seeds.

PREP: 1 MINUTE   COOK: 6 MINUTES   MAKES ABOUT 1/2 CUP

1/4 cup white sesame seeds   **1 tablespoon kosher salt**
1/4 cup black sesame seeds

In 10-inch skillet, combine white and black sesame seeds. Cook, stirring frequently, over medium heat until white sesame seeds have lightly browned, 6 to 8 minutes. Transfer to serving bowl; cool. Stir in kosher salt.

Each teaspoon: About 15 calories, 1g protein, 1g carbohydrate, 2g total fat (0g saturated), 0g fiber, 0mg cholesterol, 145mg sodium.

Artichoke Dip

Serve this simple dip with toasted pita bread. An assortment of olives and cherry tomatoes is also a nice accompaniment.

PREP: 10 MINUTES MAKES ABOUT 1 1/4 CUPS

1 lemon
1 can (13 3/4 ounces) artichoke
    hearts, drained
1/4 cup light mayonnaise

1/4 cup freshly grated Parmesan
    cheese
2 tablespoons olive oil

1. From lemon, grate 1/2 teaspoon peel and squeeze 2 teaspoons juice.
2. In food processor with knife blade attached, combine lemon peel and juice, artichoke hearts, mayonnaise, Parmesan, and oil; puree until smooth. Transfer dip to small bowl. Cover and refrigerate up to 3 days if not serving right away.

Each tablespoon: About 30 calories, 1g protein, 1g carbohydrate, 3g total fat (1g saturated), 0g fiber, 2mg cholesterol, 70mg sodium.

Artichoke Dip

Sunchoke Relish

Serve this with melba toasts spread with cream cheese or as the centerpiece of your holiday relish tray: Arrange assorted olives, baby carrots, celery sticks, radishes, and cottage cheese on a platter and place on the dinner table so guests can help themselves throughout the meal.

PREP: 30 MINUTES   COOK: 45 MINUTES   MAKES ABOUT 5 1/2 CUPS

1 pound sunchokes (Jerusalem artichokes), well scrubbed and chopped
3 large stalks celery, chopped
1 large onion, chopped
1 small red pepper, chopped

1 cup cider vinegar
1/2 cup sugar
1 tablespoon dry mustard
1 teaspoon salt
1/8 teaspoon ground cloves

1. In 4-quart saucepan, combine sunchokes, celery, onion, red pepper, vinegar, sugar, dry mustard, salt, and cloves; heat to boiling over high heat. Reduce heat to medium-low; simmer, covered, 15 minutes, stirring occasionally. Uncover and simmer, stirring occasionally, until most of liquid has evaporated, about 25 minutes longer.

2. Spoon into serving bowl; cover and refrigerate until well chilled, about 3 hours or up to 2 weeks.

Each 1/4 cup: About 40 calories, 1g protein, 9g carbohydrate, 0g total fat, 1g fiber, 0mg cholesterol, 110mg sodium.

Classic Onion Dip

At dinner parties in the 1950s, cream cheese–based onion and clam dips were two of the most popular offerings. In 1952, the Lipton Soup Company made preparing onion dip even easier by developing a dehydrated onion-soup mix. But it was a home cook who apparently created the dip that used the soup mix that became known as California Dip. Our onion dip is even better, for it's made the old-fashioned way: from slow-simmered onions folded into—of course—sour cream.

PREP: 10 MINUTES PLUS COOLING   COOK: 30 MINUTES
MAKES 1^2/3 CUPS

2 large onions (12 ounces each), finely chopped (2 cups)	1/4 teaspoon dried thyme
1 tablespoon minced garlic	1 teaspoon red wine vinegar
1 can (14 1/2 ounces) chicken broth	1 cup sour cream
1/4 cup water	1/8 teaspoon salt
1/2 bay leaf	1/8 teaspoon ground black pepper
	crackers or potato chips

1. In 2-quart saucepan, combine onions, garlic, broth, water, bay leaf, and thyme; heat to boiling over high heat. Reduce heat and cook until liquid has almost completely evaporated, about 25 minutes.

2. Transfer mixture to medium bowl; stir in vinegar. Cool to room temperature.

3. Stir in sour cream, salt, and pepper. Cover and refrigerate up to overnight. Serve with crackers or potato chips.

Each tablespoon: About 27 calories, 1g protein, 2g carbohydrate, 2g total fat (1g saturated), 0g fiber, 4mg cholesterol, 93mg sodium.

Triple Onion Dip

Yellow onions, green onions, and shallots are cooked until tender and sweet for this better-than-store-bought creamy dip. Serve with baby carrots and crispy potato chips.

PREP: 25 MINUTES PLUS CHILLING COOK: 12 MINUTES
MAKES ABOUT 3 CUPS

1 tablespoon olive oil
1 large yellow onion (12 ounces), finely chopped
2 medium shallots, finely chopped
2 green onions, thinly sliced
1 teaspoon salt

1/2 teaspoon ground black pepper
1/2 cup (about half 8-ounce container) whipped cream cheese
3/4 cup reduced-fat sour cream
3/4 cup light mayonnaise
1 1/2 teaspoons hot pepper sauce

1. In nonstick 12-inch skillet, heat oil over medium heat until hot. Add yellow onion and shallots and cook, covered, stirring occasionally, until tender and golden, 10 to 12 minutes.

2. Wrap 1 tablespoon green onion in plastic wrap and set aside in refrigerator. Add remaining green onions, salt, and pepper to skillet; cook, uncovered, stirring occasionally, until tender, about 2 minutes. Transfer onion mixture to medium bowl; refrigerate until cool.

3. In medium bowl, with wire whisk, mix cream cheese, sour cream, and mayonnaise until blended. Add cooled onion mixture and hot pepper sauce; stir to blend. Cover and refrigerate up to 2 days if not serving right away.

4. To serve, transfer dip to serving bowl; sprinkle with reserved green onion.

Each tablespoon: About 30 calories, 0g protein, 1g carbohydrate, 3g total fat (1g saturated), 0g fiber, 6mg cholesterol, 90mg sodium.

Triple Onion Dip

Margarita Mustard

Use sparingly as a dip for egg rolls, smoked salmon, Chinese dumplings, or broiled chicken wings.

PREP: 5 MINUTES MAKES ABOUT 1 CUP

1 lime
1 jar (7 to 8 ounces) grainy Dijon
  mustard with seeds

2 tablespoons honey
2 tablespoons tequila
1/8 teaspoon salt

From lime, grate 1 teaspoon peel and squeeze 2 tablespoons juice; place in small bowl. With wire whisk, mix in mustard, honey, tequila, and salt until smooth. If not serving right away, cover and refrigerate up to 1 week.

Each teaspoon: About 10 calories, 0g protein, 1g carbohydrate, 0g total fat, 0g fiber, 0mg cholesterol, 35mg sodium.

Plum and Five-Spice Sauce

Great with egg rolls, dumplings, pot stickers, or boiled shrimp.

PREP: 5 MINUTES MAKES ABOUT 1 CUP

1 jar (12 ounces) plum jam or
  preserves
2 tablespoons soy sauce

1 tablespoon seasoned rice vinegar
1/2 teaspoon Chinese five-spice
  powder

In small bowl, with wire whisk, mix jam, soy sauce, vinegar, and five-spice powder until well combined. If not serving right away, cover and refrigerate up to 1 week. To serve, let stand 30 minutes at room temperature.

Each teaspoon: About 20 calories, 0g protein, 5g carbohydrate, 0g total fat, 0g fiber, 0mg cholesterol, 55mg sodium.

Cajun Rémoulade Sauce

Try this piquant sauce as a dip for your favorite fresh vegetables.

PREP: 5 MINUTES MAKES ABOUT 1/2 CUP

1/3 cup light mayonnaise
2 tablespoons chili sauce
2 teaspoons spicy brown mustard
1 teaspoon Worcestershire sauce

2 green onions, minced, plus sliced
  green onion
1/8 teaspoon ground red pepper
  (cayenne)

In small bowl, combine mayonnaise, chili sauce, mustard, Worcestershire, minced green onion, and ground red pepper. Cover and refrigerate up to 3 days. To serve, sprinkle with sliced green onion.

Each tablespoon: About 40 calories, 0g protein, 2g carbohydrate, 3g total fat (1g saturated), 0g fiber, 3mg cholesterol, 150mg sodium.

Cucumber Salsa

This fresh-tasting—and nonfat—condiment is excellent with fish and doubles as a flavorful dip for tortilla chips.

PREP: 10 MINUTES MAKES ABOUT 1 CUP

1 lime
1 Kirby cucumber (6 ounces), peeled
  and coarsely chopped (1/2 cup)

3/4 cup bottled mild salsa
2 tablespoons chopped fresh cilantro

1. From lime, grate 1 teaspoon peel and squeeze 2 tablespoons juice.
2. In small bowl, combine lime peel and juice, cucumber, salsa, and cilantro. Cover and refrigerate up to 1 day if not serving right away.

Each tablespoon: About 5 calories, 0g protein, 1g carbohydrate, 0g total fat, 0g fiber, 0mg cholesterol, 25mg sodium.

Tangy Sauce for Meatballs

Serve this piquant sauce as a dipper for easy-to-heat frozen meatballs. Be sure to provide lots of cocktail picks.

PREP: 5 MINUTES   COOK: 8 MINUTES   MAKES ABOUT 3/4 CUP

1 bottle (12 ounces) chili sauce	2 tablespoons cider vinegar
3/4 cup water	1 tablespoon Worcestershire sauce
1/4 cup packed brown sugar	1 teaspoon dry mustard

In 1-quart saucepan, combine chili sauce, water, brown sugar, vinegar, Worcestershire, and dry mustard; heat to boiling over medium-high heat, stirring occasionally. Reduce heat to medium-low; simmer 5 minutes. Serve warm.

Each tablespoon: About 63 calories, 1g protein, 18g carbohydrate, 1g total fat (0g saturated), 0g fiber, 0mg cholesterol, 29mg sodium.

Tomato-Ginger Relish

Serve this tasty relish warm or cold with shrimp instead of the more usual red cocktail sauce.

PREP: 10 MINUTES COOK: 30 MINUTES MAKES ABOUT 2 CUPS

2 teaspoons vegetable oil
1 small onion, chopped
2 tablespoons grated, peeled fresh
  ginger
1 large garlic clove, minced
2 tablespoons water

1 can (28 ounces) diced tomatoes,
  drained
1/4 cup red wine vinegar
2 tablespoons brown sugar
1/4 teaspoon salt

1. In 2-quart saucepan, heat oil over medium heat until hot. Add onion, ginger, garlic, and water; cook, stirring frequently, until onion is very tender, about 10 minutes.

2. Stir tomatoes, vinegar, brown sugar, and salt into onion mixture; cook, stirring occasionally, until relish has thickened, about 20 minutes. Serve warm, or cover and refrigerate up to 1 week. Serve cold, or reheat to serve warm.

Each tablespoon: About 10 calories, 0g protein, 2g carbohydrate, 0g total fat, 0g fiber, 0mg cholesterol, 115mg sodium.

Warm Cheese Dip
with Salsa Verde

PREP: 5 MINUTES   MICROWAVE: 1 MINUTE   MAKES ABOUT 2 CUPS

1 package (8 ounces) Neufchâtel

1 cup bottled mild or medium green
salsa (salsa verde), at room
temperature

1/2 cup loosely packed fresh cilantro
leaves, chopped

tortilla chips

breadsticks

carrot and celery sticks

red pepper strips

1. Cut Neufchâtel into 10 equal pieces and transfer to microwave-safe 8-inch quiche or gratin dish. Cook, uncovered, in microwave on High 1 minute.

2. To serve, pour salsa over cheese; sprinkle with cilantro. Serve with tortilla chips, breadsticks, carrot and celery sticks, and red pepper strips.

Each tablespoon dip: About 20 calories, 1g protein, 1g carbohydrate, 2g total fat (1g saturated), 0g fiber, 5mg cholesterol, 50mg sodium.

Easy Aïoli

This garlicky mayonnaise (pronounced ay-OH-lee) makes a wonderful dip for vegetables and seafood or a tasty sauce for fish or lamb. It is also the traditional condiment for bouillabaisse.

PREP: 5 MINUTES   COOK: 20 MINUTES   MAKES ABOUT 3/4 CUP

1 head garlic, separated into cloves
  but not peeled (about 14 cloves)
1 1/8 teaspoons salt
1/2 cup mayonnaise
2 teaspoons fresh lemon juice

1/2 teaspoon Dijon mustard
1/8 teaspoon ground red pepper
  (cayenne)
1/4 cup extravirgin olive oil

1. In 1-quart saucepan, place garlic and 1 teaspoon salt; add enough *water* to cover by 1 inch. Cover saucepan; heat to boiling over high heat. Reduce heat to medium-low; cook until garlic softens, about 15 minutes; drain.

2. When cool enough to handle, squeeze soft garlic from each clove into blender. Add mayonnaise, lemon juice, mustard, ground red pepper, and remaining 1/8 teaspoon salt to blender. With blender running, add oil in slow, steady stream until mixture is thickened and creamy, occasionally stopping blender and scraping down sides with rubber spatula. Transfer to serving bowl. If not serving right away, cover and refrigerate up to 1 day.

Each tablespoon: About 110 calories, 0g protein, 2g carbohydrate, 12g total fat (2g saturated), 0g fiber, 5mg cholesterol, 95mg sodium.

Cucumber—Blue Cheese Dip

PREP: 5 MINUTES   MAKES ABOUT 1²/₃ CUPS

1 package (3 ounces) cream cheese, softened
1/2 English (seedless) cucumber, not peeled, cut into 1-inch pieces (about 1¹/₂ cups)
1/2 cup refrigerated bottled blue cheese salad dressing
green onions
radishes
toasted pita bread wedges

1. In food processor with knife blade attached, combine cream cheese and cucumber; pulse until cucumber is coarsely chopped.

2. Transfer cucumber mixture to serving bowl; stir in dressing until combined. If not serving right away, cover and refrigerate up to 4 hours. (If prepared more than 4 hours ahead, cucumber may cause dip to become watery.) Serve with green onions, radishes, and pita bread wedges.

Each tablespoon: About 35 calories, 1g protein, 1g carbohydrate, 4g total fat (1g saturated), 0g fiber, 4mg cholesterol, 60mg sodium.

Roasted Eggplant Dip with Herbs

The fresh flavors of lemon and mint are a perfect match for the roasted eggplant in this Mediterranean-style dip.

PREP: 15 MINUTES PLUS COOLING AND DRAINING   ROAST: 1 HOUR
MAKES ABOUT 2 CUPS

2 small eggplants (1 pound each)	1/4 teaspoon ground black pepper
2 garlic cloves, thinly sliced	2 tablespoons chopped fresh parsley
2 tablespoons olive oil	2 tablespoons chopped fresh mint
4 teaspoons fresh lemon juice	toasted pita bread wedges
1 teaspoon salt	

1. Preheat oven to 400°F. Line jelly-roll pan with foil.
2. With knife, cut slits all over eggplants; insert garlic slices in slits. Place eggplants in prepared pan and roast until collapsed and tender, about 1 hour.
3. When cool enough to handle, cut eggplants lengthwise in half. Scoop out flesh and place in colander set over bowl; discard skin. Let drain 10 minutes.
4. In food processor with knife blade attached, combine eggplant, oil, lemon juice, salt, and pepper; pulse to coarsely chop. Add parsley and mint; pulse to combine. Spoon into serving bowl; cover and refrigerate up to 4 hours. Serve with pita bread wedges.

Each tablespoon: About 14 calories, 0g protein, 2g carbohydrate, 1g total fat (0g saturated), 1g fiber, 0mg cholesterol, 74mg sodium.

Baba Ganoush

Prepare as directed but omit parsley and mint. Stir in 1/2 **teaspoon ground cumin** and 1/4 **cup plain low-fat yogurt**.

Seven-Layer Tex-Mex Dip

This dip appeared at practically every party in Texas in the early 1980s. Count the layers (there were usually seven): bean dip, mashed avocados, sour cream, green onions, chopped tomatoes, black olives, and a generous topping of shredded cheese. For our recipe, you can assemble the bean and cheese layers and guacamole separately and then refrigerate. To serve, warm the bean and cheese layers through and top with the guacamole and sour cream.

PREP: 35 MINUTES BAKE: 15 MINUTES MAKES 24 SERVINGS

1 can (15 to 19 ounces) pinto beans, rinsed and drained
1 cup bottled mild to medium salsa
2 green onions, finely chopped
1 small garlic clove, minced
4 ounces Monterey Jack cheese, shredded (1 cup)
1 can (2 1/4 ounces) sliced ripe black olives, rinsed and drained

2 ripe medium Hass avocados
1/3 cup chopped fresh cilantro
3 tablespoons finely chopped red onion
2 tablespoons fresh lime juice
1/2 teaspoon salt
1 cup sour cream
tortilla chips

1. Preheat oven to 350°F. In medium bowl, combine beans, 3 tablespoons salsa, half of green onions, and garlic. Mash until well combined but still slightly chunky. Spread in bottom of 9-inch glass pie plate.
2. Sprinkle Jack cheese over bean mixture; spread with remaining salsa and sprinkle with olives. Bake until heated through, about 15 minutes.
3. Meanwhile, cut each avocado in half and remove pit. With spoon, scoop out flesh and place in same bowl. With fork, mash avocado until slightly chunky. Stir in 1/4 cup cilantro, red onion, lime juice, and salt. Spoon avocado mixture over hot dip; spread sour cream on top. Sprinkle with remaining green onions and remaining cilantro. Serve with tortilla chips.

Each serving: About 83 calories, 3g protein, 4g carbohydrate, 6g total fat (2g saturated), 3g fiber, 9mg cholesterol, 206mg sodium.

Tzatziki

In Greece, tzatziki is served as a dip with pita bread or as a cold sauce to accompany grilled lamb, fish, or chicken.

PREP: 20 MINUTES PLUS OVERNIGHT TO DRAIN AND CHILLING
MAKES ABOUT 1 1/4 CUPS

1 container (16 ounces) plain low-fat yogurt
1/2 English (seedless) cucumber, not peeled, finely chopped plus a few very thin slices
1 1/2 teaspoons salt
1 garlic clove, chopped
1 tablespoon chopped fresh mint or dill plus additional sprigs
1 tablespoon extravirgin olive oil
1/2 teaspoon red wine vinegar
1/4 teaspoon ground black pepper

1. Spoon yogurt into sieve lined with cheesecloth or coffee filter set over bowl; cover and refrigerate overnight. Transfer drained yogurt to medium bowl; discard liquid.

2. Meanwhile, in colander set over bowl, toss chopped cucumber with 1 teaspoon salt. Let drain at least 1 hour at room temperature, or cover and refrigerate up to 8 hours. In batches, wrap chopped cucumber in clean kitchen towel and squeeze to remove as much liquid as possible. Pat cucumber dry with paper towels; add to yogurt in bowl.

3. With flat side of chef's knife, mash garlic to a paste with remaining 1/2 teaspoon salt. Add garlic, chopped mint, oil, vinegar, and pepper to yogurt; stir to combine. Cover and refrigerate at least 2 or up to 4 hours. Serve chilled or at room temperature, topped with cucumber slices and mint sprigs.

Each tablespoon: About 17 calories, 1g protein, 1g carbohydrate, 1g total fat (0g saturated), 0g fiber, 1mg cholesterol, 182mg sodium.

Hummus

Middle Eastern dips, such as hummus, once seemed exotic, but now they're familiar old friends. Tahini is readily available at health food stores and supermarkets.

PREP: 15 MINUTES PLUS CHILLING MAKES 2 CUPS

4 garlic cloves, peeled
1 large lemon
1 can (15 to 19 ounces) garbanzo beans, rinsed and drained
2 tablespoons tahini (sesame seed paste)
3 tablespoons olive oil
2 tablespoons water

1/2 teaspoon salt
1/8 teaspoon ground red pepper (cayenne)
1/2 teaspoon paprika
2 tablespoons chopped fresh cilantro (optional)
pita bread wedges
olives

1. In 1-quart saucepan, heat *2 cups water* to boiling over high heat. Add garlic and cook 3 minutes to blanch; drain.

2. From lemon, grate 1 teaspoon peel and squeeze 3 tablespoons juice. In food processor with knife blade attached, combine beans, tahini, garlic, lemon peel and juice, oil, water, salt, and ground red pepper; puree until smooth. Transfer to platter; cover and refrigerate up to 4 hours. To serve, sprinkle with paprika and cilantro, if using. Serve with pita bread wedges and olives.

Each tablespoon: About 28 calories, 1g protein, 2g carbohydrate, 2g total fat (0g saturated), 1g fiber, 0mg cholesterol, 54mg sodium.

Meze

L ittle savory dishes to be nibbled before a meal or with drinks, meze are a tradition in Greece, Turkey, and the Middle East. Try any of the following dips with pita or French bread, along with feta cheese chunks, olives, radishes, sliced cucumbers, or tomato wedges: Roasted Red Pepper and Walnut Dip, Tzatziki, Hummus, or Roasted Eggplant Dip with Herbs.

Herbed Yogurt-Cheese Dip

Drained yogurt has a thick, cheeselike consistency. Drain it the day before you make the dip. The longer it drains, the thicker the "cheese" will be. If you like, substitute fresh parsley or cilantro for the basil.

PREP: 10 MINUTES PLUS OVERNIGHT TO DRAIN   COOK: 5 MINUTES
MAKES 1 CUP

1 1/2 cups plain low-fat yogurt
2 garlic cloves, peeled
3/4 cup finely chopped fresh basil
2 teaspoons olive oil

1/2 teaspoon salt
assorted crackers or cut-up
  vegetables

1. Place yogurt in sieve lined with cheesecloth or coffee filter set over bowl; cover and refrigerate overnight. Transfer drained yogurt to bowl; discard liquid.

2. In 1-quart saucepan, heat *2 cups water* to boiling over high heat. Add garlic and cook 3 minutes to blanch; drain. With flat side of chef's knife, mash garlic; add to yogurt. Stir in basil, oil, and salt. Cover and refrigerate up to 4 hours. Serve with crackers or cut-up vegetables.

Each tablespoon: About 17 calories, 1g protein, 1g carbohydrate, 1g total fat (0g saturated), 0g fiber, 1mg cholesterol, 79mg sodium.

Moroccan Dip

Serve with an assortment of crudités such as endive, baby carrots, blanched asparagus, or sliced peppers, or our Pistachio-Sesame Pita Crisps (page 85).

(page 85)

PREP: 15 MINUTES   COOK: 2 MINUTES   MAKES ABOUT 1 1/2 CUPS

1 teaspoon paprika
1/4 teaspoon fennel seeds, crushed
1/4 teaspoon ground ginger
1/4 teaspoon ground cumin
1/8 teaspoon ground red pepper
  (cayenne)
1 can (15 to 19 ounces) garbanzo
  beans, rinsed and drained

1/4 cup water
2 tablespoons olive oil
2 tablespoons fresh lemon juice
1/2 teaspoon salt
1/4 teaspoon ground black pepper

1. In 8-inch skillet, combine paprika, fennel seeds, ginger, cumin, and ground red pepper. Cook, stirring constantly, over medium-low heat until spices are fragrant and lightly toasted, 1 to 2 minutes; remove from heat.

2. In food processor with knife blade attached, combine beans, water, oil, lemon juice, salt, black pepper, and toasted spices; puree until smooth. Transfer to serving bowl. Cover and refrigerate up to 3 days if not serving right away.

Each tablespoon: About 40 calories, 1g protein, 5g carbohydrate, 1g total fat (0g saturated), 1g fiber, 0mg cholesterol, 90mg sodium.

Bagna Cauda

The slow simmering of peeled garlic cloves gives this dip its rich garlic flavor and suave texture—without any bite. While some bagna caudas are olive oil–based, this one is creamy. The name is a derivation of *bagna caldo*, which means "hot bath" in Italian. Serve warm with a platter of cool, crisp vegetables.

PREP: 10 MINUTES   COOK: 27 MINUTES   MAKES 2/3 CUP

2/3 **cup heavy or whipping cream**
1/4 **cup peeled garlic cloves (from 1**
  small head garlic)

1 **teaspoon anchovy paste**
1/8 **teaspoon ground red pepper**
  (cayenne)

1. In 1-quart saucepan, combine cream and garlic; heat to boiling over medium-low heat. Reduce heat to low; simmer, covered, until garlic is very soft, about 25 minutes.

2. In food processor with knife blade attached, combine garlic-cream mixture, anchovy paste, and ground red pepper; puree until smooth and thick. Serve warm.

Each tablespoon: About 37 calories, 1g protein, 2g carbohydrate, 3g total fat (2g saturated), 0g fiber, 14mg cholesterol, 39mg sodium.

Peanut-Ginger Dip

Can't get your kids to eat their veggies? Set out crispy carrot, celery, and cucumber sticks with this super creamy dip. You can make it early in the day, but leave it out at room temperature (the mixture will get too stiff if refrigerated).

PREP: 10 MINUTES MAKES ABOUT 1 1/4 CUPS

3/4 cup creamy peanut butter
1/3 cup boiling water
1/4 cup honey

4 teaspoons soy sauce
1 teaspoon grated, peeled fresh
  ginger

In medium bowl, with wire whisk, mix peanut butter, boiling water, honey, soy sauce, and ginger until smooth.

Each tablespoon: About 71 calories, 2g protein, 5g carbohydrate, 5g total fat (1g saturated), 1g fiber, 0mg cholesterol, 71mg sodium.

Red Caviar Dip

Bright and tangy, this can be put together in a flash. Serve with bagel chips, crisp celery, or other vegetables of choice.

PREP: 5 MINUTES MAKES ABOUT 2 CUPS

2 packages (3 ounces each) cream
  cheese, softened
2/3 cup sour cream

1 jar (2 ounces) red lumpfish caviar,
  undrained
1 teaspoon fresh lemon juice

In medium bowl, with wooden spoon or rubber spatula, mash cream cheese. Gently stir in sour cream, caviar, and lemon juice until blended.

Each tablespoon: About 33 calories, 1g protein, 1g carbohydrate, 3g total fat (2g saturated), 0g fiber, 18mg cholesterol, 45mg sodium.

Caviar Pie

Fast and festive, this "pie" is perfect party fare. Serve with plain crackers.

PREP: 20 MINUTES COOK: 10 MINUTES PLUS STANDING
MAKES ABOUT 3 CUPS

8 large eggs

1/3 cup mayonnaise

1/4 cup chopped fresh dill or parsley

1 container (8 ounces) sour cream

1/4 teaspoon salt

1/4 teaspoon ground black pepper

1 jar (2 ounces) red lumpfish caviar

1. In 3-quart saucepan, place eggs and enough *cold water* to cover by at least 1 inch; heat to boiling over high heat. Immediately remove saucepan from heat and cover tightly; let stand 15 minutes. Pour off hot water and run cold water over eggs to cool. Peel eggs.

2. In medium bowl, with potato masher or large fork, mash eggs. Stir in mayonnaise, dill, 2 tablespoons sour cream, salt, and pepper. Spoon egg mixture evenly into 9-inch pie plate. Cover and refrigerate up to 4 hours until ready to serve.

3. To serve, spread remaining sour cream evenly over pie; spoon caviar over top.

Each tablespoon: About 33 calories, 1g protein, 1g carbohydrate, 3g total fat (1g saturated), 0g fiber, 49mg cholesterol, 30mg sodium.

Green Goddess Dip

Created in the 1920s at San Francisco's Palace Hotel, the original green goddess dressing was named in honor of actor George Arliss, who was appearing in a play entitled "Green Goddess." When blanched, garlic becomes mellow, making it possible to infuse its delicious flavor into food without the bite. If you prefer, substitute reduced-fat sour cream for the regular.

PREP: 8 MINUTES COOK: 3 MINUTES MAKES 3/4 CUP

1 teaspoon dried tarragon
2 teaspoons fresh lemon juice
2 garlic cloves, peeled
1/2 cup sour cream

1/2 cup chopped fresh parsley
2 green onions, finely chopped
2 tablespoons light mayonnaise
1 1/2 teaspoons anchovy paste

1. In medium bowl, combine tarragon and lemon juice.

2. In 1-quart saucepan, heat *2 cups water* to boiling over high heat. Add garlic, and cook 3 minutes to blanch; drain. With flat side of chef's knife, mash garlic to paste; add to tarragon mixture in bowl. Stir in sour cream, parsley, green onions, mayonnaise, and anchovy paste until well mixed.

Each tablespoon: About 52 calories, 1g protein, 4g carbohydrate, 4g total fat (2g saturated), 1g fiber, 10mg cholesterol, 81mg sodium.

Skordalia

Serve this Greek potato-based dip with crunchy green beans, and carrot and celery sticks. Tasty walnuts thicken this version and give it rich, full flavor.

PREP: 10 MINUTES   COOK: 20 MINUTES   MAKES ABOUT 1²/3 CUPS

2 medium all-purpose potatoes (12 ounces), peeled and thinly sliced
6 garlic cloves, peeled
³/4 teaspoon salt

¹/2 cup walnuts, toasted
2 tablespoons extravirgin olive oil
2 teaspoons fresh lemon juice

1. In 2-quart saucepan, combine potatoes, garlic, ¹/4 teaspoon salt, and *3 cups water;* heat to boiling over medium heat. Cook until potatoes are fork-tender, 10 to 12 minutes. Drain, reserving *3 tablespoons cooking water.*
2. Meanwhile, in food processor with knife blade attached, puree walnuts, oil, and lemon juice until smooth.
3. Transfer potatoes, garlic, and reserved cooking water to medium bowl. With potato masher, mash mixture until smooth. Stir in walnut mixture and remaining ¹/2 teaspoon salt until well combined.

Each tablespoon: About 37 calories, 1g protein, 3g carbohydrate, 3g total fat (1g saturated), 1g fiber, 0mg cholesterol, 1mg sodium.

Taramasalata

Sometimes taramasalata is made with potato and sometimes not; with this versatile recipe, you can prepare it either way. If you'd like to use potato, peel and cut one small all-purpose potato (about four ounces) into half-inch pieces. While the tarama is soaking, combine the potato with enough *cold water* to cover and heat to boiling. Cook until tender. Drain the potato and put through food mill or ricer while hot, then set aside to cool. (Don't do this in the food processor or the potato will become gummy.) Stir into the taramasalata when cool.

PREP: 30 MINUTES   MAKES ABOUT 1 CUP

3/4 cup tarama (carp, mullet, or cod roe)

1 small green onion (white part only), finely chopped, plus whole green onions

2 to 3 tablespoons fresh lemon juice

pinch ground black pepper

3/4 cup olive oil or more as needed

Kalamata olives

radishes

lemon wedges

cucumber slices

warm pita bread

1. In bowl, soak tarama in enough *cold water* to cover 15 minutes, breaking up any lumps. Drain tarama through fine mesh sieve or sieve lined with damp cheesecloth, pressing with back of spoon to remove as much salty water as possible. Discard water.

2. In food processor fitted with knife blade, combine drained tarama, finely chopped green onion, 2 tablespoons lemon juice, and pepper; puree until pale, creamy, and smooth, about 3 minutes. With processor running, add oil in slow, steady stream; puree until creamy.

3. Transfer taramasalata to serving bowl. Taste and adjust seasoning; add more oil to make it creamier or more lemon juice to make it sharper, if you like. Serve with olives, radishes, lemon wedges, cucumber slices, and warm pita bread.

Each tablespoon: About 105 calories, 2g protein, 1g carbohydrate, 11g total fat (1g saturated), 0g fiber, 7mg cholesterol, 6mg sodium.

Curry Dip

Mango chutney gives this dip a slight kick and a touch of sweetness. For a lower-fat dip, substitute Neufchâtel and reduced-fat sour cream for the regular versions. Serve with crunchy vegetables.

PREP: 5 MINUTES   MAKES $3/4$ CUP

1 package (3 ounces) cream cheese
1/4 cup sour cream
2 tablespoons mango chutney
1 teaspoon curry powder

1/2 teaspoon ground coriander
1/4 teaspoon ground cumin
1/4 teaspoon ground ginger
1/4 teaspoon salt

In food processor with knife blade attached, combine cream cheese, sour cream, chutney, curry powder, coriander, cumin, ginger, and salt; puree until smooth. Transfer to serving bowl. Cover and refrigerate up to 4 hours.

Each tablespoon: About 44 calories, 1g protein, 1g carbohydrate, 4g total fat (1g saturated), 0g fiber, 0mg cholesterol, 27mg sodium.

Soy Dipping Sauce

This is the perfect dipping sauce for grilled chicken strips, grilled or broiled shrimp, and your favorite dumplings or pot stickers. Make a double batch; it holds up well in the refrigerator.

PREP: 5 MINUTES   MAKES ABOUT $1/2$ CUP

1/4 cup soy sauce
1/4 cup seasoned rice vinegar or white wine vinegar

2 tablespoons peeled fresh ginger, cut into very thin slivers

In small serving bowl, combine soy sauce, vinegar, and ginger.

Each teaspoon: About 4 calories, 0g protein, 1g carbohydrate, 0g total fat, 0g fiber, 0mg cholesterol, 221mg sodium.

Alaskan Salmon Spread

Fresh and smoked salmon are a winning combination. This spread is ideal party food as it can be prepared up to two days ahead.

PREP: 30 MINUTES PLUS CHILLING COOK: 8 MINUTES
MAKES ABOUT 2 1/2 CUPS

salt
1 salmon fillet (8 ounces), skin removed
1 lemon
8 ounces smoked salmon, finely chopped
1/2 cup butter or margarine (1 stick), softened
2 tablespoons plus 1 teaspoon chopped fresh chives
1 teaspoon Dijon mustard
1 teaspoon capers, drained and chopped
1/8 teaspoon coarsely ground black pepper
sliced French bread

1. In 10-inch skillet, combine *4 cups water* and 1 teaspoon salt; heat to boiling over high heat. Add salmon fillet; heat to boiling. Reduce heat to low; cover and simmer until salmon flakes easily when tested with fork, 8 to 10 minutes. With slotted spatula, carefully transfer salmon to paper towels to drain, still holding fish on spatula. Place salmon in medium bowl; cool slightly.

2. Meanwhile, from lemon grate 1 teaspoon peel and squeeze 2 tablespoons juice.

3. With wooden spoon, mash salmon almost to smooth paste. Add smoked salmon, butter, 2 tablespoons chopped chives, lemon peel and juice, mustard, capers, and pepper; blend thoroughly.

4. Spoon salmon mixture into crock or serving bowl. Cover and refrigerate at least 2 hours. To serve, let stand 30 minutes at room temperature, or until soft enough to spread. Sprinkle with remaining 1 teaspoon chives and serve with sliced French bread.

Each tablespoon without bread: About 35 calories, 2g protein, 0g carbohydrate, 3g total fat (1g saturated), 0g fiber, 5mg cholesterol, 90mg sodium.

Alaskan Salmon Spread

Potted Shrimp

This old-fashioned recipe is a specialty in the Carolinas, where each family's rendition is cherished.

PREP: 15 MINUTES PLUS CHILLING   COOK: 3 MINUTES
MAKES ABOUT 2 CUPS

8 tablespoons unsalted butter (1 stick), softened
1 pound medium shrimp, shelled and deveined
3/4 teaspoon salt
1/4 teaspoon ground red pepper (cayenne)
2 tablespoons dry sherry
sesame crackers or toast

1. In 10-inch skillet, melt 1 tablespoon butter over medium-high heat. Add shrimp, salt, and ground red pepper. Cook, stirring frequently, until shrimp are opaque throughout, about 2 minutes. Add sherry and cook 30 seconds.

2. In food processor with knife blade attached, pulse shrimp with pan juices until finely chopped. Cut remaining 7 tablespoons butter into pieces. Add to shrimp in processor; process until well combined.

3. Transfer shrimp mixture to serving bowl. Cover and refrigerate up to 24 hours. To serve, let stand 30 minutes at room temperature. Serve with sesame crackers or toast.

Each tablespoon: About 39 calories, 2g protein, 0g carbohydrate, 3g total fat (2g saturated), 0g fiber, 25mg cholesterol, 72mg sodium.

Maryland Crab Dip

In the 1950s, hostesses coast to coast entertained friends at fancy cocktail parties and informal backyard barbecues. This hot dip, made with chunks of crab, a hint of curry, and slivers of almonds, was often served regardless of what else was on the menu. Our recipe uses Old Bay seasoning instead of curry powder.

PREP: 5 MINUTES BAKE: 23 MINUTES MAKES 1 1/2 CUPS

1/3 cup slivered almonds	2 tablespoons minced onion
1/2 pound lump crabmeat, picked over	2 tablespoons chopped fresh parsley
1/2 cup mayonnaise	1 teaspoon Old Bay seasoning
1/3 cup sour cream	crackers

1. Preheat oven to 350°F. Grease 9-inch pie plate. Spread almonds on cookie sheet. Bake, stirring occasionally, until lightly browned and fragrant, about 8 minutes; cool.
2. In medium bowl, combine crabmeat, mayonnaise, sour cream, onion, parsley, and Old Bay seasoning. Turn into prepared pie plate and spread evenly.
3. Bake until heated through, about 15 minutes. Sprinkle with almonds. Serve with crackers.

Each tablespoon: About 62 calories, 2g protein, 1g carbohydrate, 6g total fat (1g saturated), 0g fiber, 14mg cholesterol, 82mg sodium.

Roasted-Garlic Spread

Roasting garlic gives it a mellow sweetness. The garlic can be roasted up to two days ahead, squeezed out of its skin, and refrigerated. Use this spread on toasted pitas, or serve as a dip for crudités.

PREP: 10 MINUTES PLUS COOLING BAKE: 50 MINUTES
MAKES ABOUT 1 1/4 CUPS

2 heads garlic (about 2 ounces each)	1 tablespoon olive oil
1/4 cup walnuts	1/2 teaspoon salt
1 container (8 ounces) sour cream	

1. Preheat oven to 400°F. Remove any loose papery skin from garlic, leaving heads intact. Place garlic on sheet of heavy-duty foil. Loosely wrap foil around garlic. Roast until garlic has softened, about 50 minutes.
2. Meanwhile, place walnuts in small baking pan. Bake, stirring once, until toasted, 7 to 10 minutes.
3. When garlic is cool enough to handle, separate into cloves. Squeeze soft garlic from each clove into small bowl; discard skin. (You should have about 1/3 cup.)
4. In food processor with knife blade attached, combine garlic, sour cream, walnuts, oil, and salt; puree until smooth. Spoon into serving bowl. Cover and refrigerate up to 3 days.

Each tablespoon: About 50 calories, 1g protein, 3g carbohydrate, 4g total fat (2g saturated), 0g fiber, 5mg cholesterol, 65mg sodium.

Green Herb Sauce

Arrange slices of roast beef on French bread rounds. Top with this delicious tangy sauce. It's great on pork and chicken appetizers too.

Prep: 10 minutes   Makes about 1/2 cup

1 cup loosely packed fresh parsley leaves	2 tablespoons water
1 cup loosely packed fresh cilantro leaves	2 teaspoons red wine vinegar
	1/2 small garlic clove
2 tablespoons olive oil	1/4 teaspoon salt
	1/8 teaspoon crushed red pepper

In mini food processor or blender, combine parsley, cilantro, oil, water, vinegar, garlic, salt, and crushed red pepper; process until herbs are very finely chopped and sauce is well blended, scraping bowl occasionally with rubber spatula. Transfer to small bowl; cover and refrigerate up to 1 day if not serving right away.

Each tablespoon: About 35 calories, 0g protein, 1g carbohydrate, 4g total fat (1g saturated), 1g fiber, 0mg cholesterol, 80mg sodium.

Roasted Red Pepper Puree

Spread this puree on slices of toasted French bread for a tasty hors d'oeuvre.

PREP: 10 MINUTES PLUS COOLING ROAST: 8 MINUTES
MAKES ABOUT 2/3 CUP

2 medium red peppers
1 slice whole-wheat or white bread,
    torn into bite-size pieces
1 tablespoon olive oil
1 tablespoon water

1/2 small garlic clove
1 teaspoon fennel seeds, crushed
1/2 teaspoon salt
1/8 teaspoon coarsely ground black
    pepper

1. Preheat broiler. Line broiling pan with foil. Cut each red pepper lengthwise in half; remove and discard stems and seeds. Arrange peppers, cut side down, in prepared pan. Place pan in broiler, 5 to 6 inches from heat source. Broil peppers, without turning, until skin is charred and blistered, 8 to 10 minutes. Wrap peppers in foil and allow to steam at room temperature 15 minutes or until cool enough to handle. Peel off skin and discard.

2. Cut roasted peppers into bite-size pieces. In mini food processor or in blender, combine red peppers, bread, oil, water, garlic, fennel seeds, salt, and black pepper. Puree until smooth, scraping bowl occasionally with rubber spatula. Transfer mixture to small bowl; cover and refrigerate up to 3 days if not serving right away.

Each tablespoon: About 25 calories, 1g protein, 3g carbohydrate, 1g total fat (0g saturated), 0g fiber, 0mg cholesterol, 120mg sodium.

Swiss Fondue

This ever-popular hot cheese specialty from Switzerland was popularized in the 1950s when Americans were discovering new "foreign" dishes. The name comes from the French word *fondre* (to melt). This classic version uses Swiss cheese, Gruyère cheese, and white wine to create the perfect balance of flavors.

PREP: 15 MINUTES   COOK: 15 MINUTES   MAKES 6 APPETIZER SERVINGS

1 garlic clove, cut in half
1 1/2 cups dry white wine
1 tablespoon kirsch or brandy
8 ounces Swiss or Emmental cheese, shredded (2 cups)
8 ounces Gruyère cheese, shredded (2 cups)

3 tablespoons all-purpose flour
1/8 teaspoon ground black pepper
pinch ground nutmeg
1 loaf (16 ounces) French bread, cut into 1-inch cubes

1. Rub inside of fondue pot or heavy, nonreactive 2-quart saucepan with garlic; discard garlic. Pour wine into fondue pot. Heat over medium-low heat until very hot but not boiling; stir in kirsch.

2. Meanwhile, in medium bowl, toss Swiss cheese, Gruyère, and flour until mixed. Add cheese mixture, one handful at a time, to wine, stirring constantly and vigorously until cheese has melted and mixture is thick and smooth. If mixture separates, increase heat to medium, stirring just until smooth. Stir in pepper and nutmeg.

3. Transfer fondue to table; place over tabletop heater to keep hot, if you like. To eat, spear cubes of French bread onto long-handled fondue forks and dip into cheese mixture.

Each serving: About 567 calories, 29g protein, 45g carbohydrate, 25g total fat (14g saturated), 0g fiber, 76mg cholesterol, 689mg sodium.

Baked Brie with Lemon and Herbs

Baked Brie with Lemon and Herbs

Here, Brie cheese is split and filled with parsley, thyme, lemon, and pepper, then baked until slightly runny and fragrant. Choose either a medium wheel or a wedge cut from a large wheel. The Brie can be assembled through step two and refrigerated up to one day ahead. About 45 minutes before serving, continue from step three.

PREP: 15 MINUTES PLUS COOLING BAKE: 15 MINUTES
MAKES 24 APPETIZER SERVINGS

1 cup loosely packed fresh parsley
  leaves, chopped
1 tablespoon fresh thyme leaves,
  finely chopped
1 teaspoon freshly grated lemon peel
1/2 teaspoon coarsely ground black
  pepper

1 wheel (2.2 pounds) cold ripe Brie
  cheese (about 7 1/2 inches in
  diameter) or one 2-pound wedge
apple wedges
grapes
assorted crackers

1. In small bowl, combine parsley, thyme, lemon peel, and pepper.
2. With long, thin knife, cut Brie horizontally in half. Lift off top layer; sprinkle parsley mixture evenly over bottom layer. Replace top layer, rind side up. Wrap Brie in foil. Let wrapped Brie stand 1 hour at room temperature.
3. Meanwhile, preheat oven to 350°F. Place wrapped Brie on small cookie sheet; bake 15 minutes. Cool Brie on cookie sheet on wire rack 20 minutes. (If served hot, cheese will be too soft and runny.) Unwrap Brie and carefully transfer to serving plate. Serve with apple wedges, grapes, and assorted crackers.

Each serving: About 140 calories, 9g protein, 0g carbohydrate, 12g total fat (7g saturated), 0g fiber, 42mg cholesterol, 265mg sodium.

Potted Cheddar and Beer Spread

The flavors in this spread were inspired by Welsh rarebit, the ever-popular British sauce made with Cheddar cheese and beer and served over toast.

PREP: 15 MINUTES PLUS CHILLING AND STANDING   MAKES 5 CUPS

1¹/₂ pounds extrasharp Cheddar
cheese, shredded (6 cups)
1 can or bottle (12 ounces) beer
6 tablespoons butter or margarine,
softened
1 tablespoon Dijon mustard

1 tablespoon Worcestershire sauce
¹/₈ teaspoon ground red pepper
(cayenne)
¹/₈ teaspoon ground nutmeg
assorted crackers

1. In large bowl, with wooden spoon, stir Cheddar cheese and beer until well blended. Let stand until cheese has softened, about 30 minutes.

2. In food processor with knife blade attached, combine cheese mixture, butter, mustard, Worcestershire, ground red pepper, and nutmeg; process until smooth, 3 to 5 minutes. Pack cheese mixture into airtight containers and store in refrigerator up to 1 month or in freezer up to 3 months.

3. To serve, let cheese mixture stand 30 minutes at room temperature, or until soft enough to spread. Serve with assorted crackers.

Each tablespoon: About 44 calories, 2g protein, 0g carbohydrate, 4g total fat (2g saturated), 0g fiber, 11mg cholesterol, 68mg sodium.

Tomato-Basil Cream Cheese Logs

Spread this Italian-inspired, cream cheese log on thinly sliced Italian bread toasts or on crackers.

PREP: 15 MINUTES PLUS SOAKING AND CHILLING
MAKES TWO 6-INCH LOGS, 12 SERVINGS EACH

1/3 **cup dried tomatoes**
2 **packages (8 ounces each) cream cheese, softened**
1/3 **cup chopped fresh basil**
1/4 **cup freshly grated Parmesan cheese**

1/2 **teaspoon coarsely ground black pepper**
1/2 **cup pine nuts (pignoli), toasted and finely chopped**

1. Soak dried tomatoes in enough *boiling water* to cover until softened, about 15 minutes. Drain tomatoes well, then finely chop.
2. In small bowl, with mixer at medium speed, beat cream cheese until light and creamy, about 1 minute. With wooden spoon, stir in tomatoes, basil, Parmesan, and pepper.
3. On waxed paper, shape half of cheese mixture into 6-inch log; roll in waxed paper, twisting ends to seal. Repeat with remaining cheese mixture. Refrigerate until chilled and firm, at least 1 hour. Roll logs in pine nuts; rewrap and refrigerate at least 15 minutes longer or up to 6 hours.

Each serving: About 90 calories, 3g protein, 2g carbohydrate, 8g total fat (5g saturated), 0g fiber, 22mg cholesterol, 76mg sodium.

Roquefort-Pecan Spread

You can prepare this spread several hours in advance. Spoon it onto endive leaves, thinly sliced apple, toasted raisin-walnut bread, or crackers.

PREP: 25 MINUTES PLUS COOLING   MAKES 1 1/2 CUPS

2 teaspoons butter or margarine
2 ripe pears, peeled and cut into
   1/2-inch pieces
1 tablespoon sugar
2 tablespoons dry sherry

4 ounces Roquefort cheese (1 cup),
   crumbled
2 ounces cream cheese, softened
1/4 cup pecans, toasted and finely
   chopped

1. In nonstick 10-inch skillet, melt butter over medium heat. Add pears and toss to coat. Add sugar and cook until pears are tender, about 4 minutes. Add sherry and cook until sherry has evaporated, about 2 minutes. Cool to room temperature.

2. In small bowl, with mixer at medium speed, beat Roquefort and cream cheese until smooth. With wooden spoon, stir in pears and pecans. Transfer to serving bowl.

Each teaspoon: About 16 calories, 1g protein, 1g carbohydrate, 1g total fat (1g saturated), 0g fiber, 3mg cholesterol, 35mg sodium.

Cream Cheese to the Rescue

Unexpected guests at your doorstep? For an almost-instant spread, place an 8-ounce package of cream cheese on a serving platter and spread generously with hot pepper jelly, mango chutney, olive paste (olivada), or salsa. Or, in a food processor with the knife blade attached, puree the cream cheese with marinated dried tomatoes, roasted peppers, pickled jalapeño chiles, prepared horseradish, or grated onion and season with coarsely ground pepper. To turn the tasty mixture into a dip, simply thin it with a bit with milk. No chips or crackers on hand? Toast some slices of bread and cut them into neat triangles.

Blue-Cheese Ball

Two kinds of cheeses are flavored up with bourbon and mustard, then coated with toasted seeds or nuts. Serve with a basket filled with your favorite crackers.

PREP: 10 MINUTES PLUS OVERNIGHT TO CHILL
MAKES 12 APPETIZER SERVINGS

1 package (8 ounces) reduced-fat
  cream cheese, softened
4 ounces blue cheese, crumbled
  (1 cup)

2 teaspoons bourbon (optional)
3/4 teaspoon dry mustard
2 tablespoons toasted sesame seeds
  or finely chopped walnuts, toasted

1. In small bowl, with mixer at medium speed, beat cream cheese and blue cheese until blended. Beat in bourbon, if using, and dry mustard. With hands, shape cheese mixture into ball. Wrap in plastic wrap and refrigerate overnight.

2. To serve, with hands reshape ball and roll in sesame seeds.

Each serving: About 85 calories, 4g protein, 1g carbohydrate, 7g total fat (4g saturated), 0g fiber, 20mg cholesterol, 211mg sodium.

Sherry–Blue Cheese Spread

PREP: 10 MINUTES   MAKES ABOUT 1 3/4 CUPS

1 green onion, cut into 2-inch pieces
1 package (8 ounces) cream cheese, softened
4 ounces blue cheese, crumbled (about 1 cup)

3 tablespoons dry sherry
assorted crackers
Belgian endive leaves
pear or apple wedges

1. In food processor with knife blade attached, pulse green onion until coarsely chopped. Add cream cheese, blue cheese, and sherry; process until smooth.

2. Transfer mixture to serving bowl. If not serving right away, cover and refrigerate up to 2 days. Serve with crackers, endive, and pear wedges.

Each tablespoon: About 45 calories, 2g protein, 1g carbohydrate, 4g total fat (3g saturated), 0g fiber, 12mg cholesterol, 80mg sodium.

Sherry–Blue Cheese Spread

Crostini with Chicken Livers and Sage

This chunky, Tuscan style pâté would also be good with thin apple or pear wedges.

PREP: 15 MINUTES   COOK: 10 MINUTES
MAKES ABOUT 30 CROSTINI

1 loaf French bread (8 ounces), cut on diagonal into thin slices
1 tablespoon butter or margarine
1 tablespoon olive oil
1 medium onion, finely chopped
1 garlic clove, finely chopped
1 pound chicken livers, each cut in half and trimmed
1/4 cup all-purpose flour
1/2 teaspoon dried sage
1/2 teaspoon salt
1/4 teaspoon ground black pepper
1 tablespoon red wine vinegar
2 tablespoons chopped fresh parsley

1. Preheat oven to 400°F. Place bread on cookie sheet and bake until lightly toasted, about 5 minutes.
2. In 10-inch skillet, melt butter with oil over medium heat. Add onion and cook, stirring frequently, until tender, about 5 minutes. Stir in garlic.
3. Meanwhile, on waxed paper, toss chicken livers with flour until coated, shaking off excess. Add chicken livers, sage, salt, and pepper to skillet. Cook, stirring, until livers are browned but still slightly pink in center, about 4 minutes. Stir in vinegar; remove from heat. Stir in parsley, mashing livers coarsely with back of spoon.
4. To serve, spread 1 tablespoon liver mixture on each toast slice.

Each crostini: 54 calories, 3g protein, 6g carbohydrate, 2g total fat (1g saturated), 0g fiber, 53mg cholesterol, 77mg sodium.

Country Pâté

A classic of French cuisine, pâté is wonderful for entertaining because it can be made so far in advance, and everyone loves it. This one has lots of flavor and less fat than standard recipes, thanks to flavorful mushrooms and moist and juicy chicken breasts. Serve with crusty bread, Dijon mustard, and cornichons (gherkins).

PREP: 50 MINUTES PLUS OVERNIGHT TO STAND
BAKE: 1 HOUR 15 MINUTES
MAKES 32 APPETIZER SERVINGS

2 large skinless, boneless chicken-breast halves (12 ounces)
3 slices bacon, finely chopped
8 ounces small white mushrooms, trimmed and finely chopped
1 medium onion, finely chopped
2 tablespoons butter or margarine
2 garlic cloves, finely chopped
2 tablespoons brandy
1 1/2 teaspoons salt

1 teaspoon ground black pepper
1 teaspoon dried thyme
1/4 teaspoon ground allspice
8 ounces ground pork
4 ounces chicken livers, trimmed and finely chopped
1/4 cup shelled pistachios
1/4 cup plus 1 tablespoon chopped fresh parsley

1. Preheat oven to 350°F. Lightly oil 8 1/2" by 4 1/2" loaf pan.
2. In a food processor with knife blade attached, process chicken until finely ground, about 30 seconds.
3. In 10-inch skillet, cook bacon over medium heat until crisp. With slotted spoon, transfer to paper towels to drain. Add mushrooms, onion, butter, and garlic to skillet; cook, stirring, until vegetables are tender, about 8 minutes. Stir in brandy, salt, pepper, thyme, and allspice. Reduce heat to low; cook 5 minutes. Transfer mixture to large plate; cool to room temperature.
4. In large bowl, combine bacon, mushroom mixture, pork, chicken, chicken livers, pistachios, and 1/4 cup parsley. With wooden spoon, beat meat mixture until very well combined.
5. Spoon mixture into prepared pan, pressing down with rubber spatula to remove any air pockets. Bake 1 hour 15 minutes. Transfer to wire rack;

cover with foil. Place another loaf pan on top of pâté; place cans inside to weight down pâté. Cool to room temperature, then refrigerate overnight (still weighted down).

6. To serve, remove cans and top loaf pan. Dip pan in hot water 15 seconds; run narrow metal spatula around sides of pan to release pâté. Invert onto cutting board. Sprinkle with remaining 1 tablespoon parsley and cut into thin slices.

Each serving: About 75 calories, 8g protein, 1g carbohydrate, 4g total fat (2g saturated), 0g fiber, 34mg cholesterol, 110mg sodium.

Smoked Trout Pâté

A smoky spread that is easily prepared in a food processor.

PREP: 30 MINUTES   MAKES ABOUT 3 CUPS

3 whole smoked trout (6 ounces each)
1 container (8 ounces) whipped cream cheese
1/4 cup low-fat mayonnaise dressing
3 tablespoons fresh lemon juice
1/8 teaspoon ground black pepper
1 tablespoon finely chopped fresh chives or green onion
cucumber slices
assorted crackers

1. Cut head and tail from each trout; discard along with skin and bones. In food processor with knife blade attached, puree trout, cream cheese, mayonnaise dressing, lemon juice, and pepper until smooth.

2. Spoon trout mixture into serving bowl; stir in chives. Cover and refrigerate up to overnight if not serving right away. To serve, let stand 15 minutes at room temperature to soften. Serve with cucumber slices and assorted crackers.

Each tablespoon: About 35 calories, 2g protein, 1g carbohydrate, 3g total fat (1g saturated), 0g fiber, 7mg cholesterol, 100mg sodium.

Chicken Liver Pâté

The more Americans traveled overseas in the 1960s and 1970s, the more they developed a taste for sophisticated foods such as French pâté. Our silky smooth version is seasoned the traditional way: with a splash of brandy, some black pepper, and dried thyme.

PREP: 25 MINUTES PLUS CHILLING COOK: 23 MINUTES
MAKES ABOUT 1 1/2 CUPS

2 tablespoons butter or margarine
1 small onion, finely chopped
1 garlic clove, finely chopped
1 pound chicken livers, trimmed
2 tablespoons brandy
1/2 cup heavy or whipping cream

1/2 teaspoon salt
1/4 teaspoon dried thyme
1/4 teaspoon ground black pepper
assorted crackers or toast triangles
thinly sliced apples

1. In 10-inch skillet, melt butter over medium-high heat. Add onion; cook, stirring frequently, until tender and golden, about 10 minutes. Stir in garlic and chicken livers; cook until livers are lightly browned but still pink inside, about 5 minutes. Stir in brandy; cook 5 minutes longer.

2. In blender or in food processor with knife blade attached, combine chicken liver mixture, cream, salt, thyme, and pepper; puree until smooth, scraping down sides of blender with rubber spatula.

3. Spoon mixture into serving bowl; cover and refrigerate at least 3 hours or up to overnight. To serve, let stand 30 minutes at room temperature. Serve with assorted crackers, toast, or thinly sliced apples.

Each tablespoon: About 54 calories, 4g protein, 1g carbohydrate, 4g total fat (2g saturated), 0g fiber, 92mg cholesterol, 75mg sodium.

Cheese Torta

Make this green, white, and red Italian flag–colored torta a day or two ahead so it has time to firm and for its flavors to blend. Molded in a bowl, it's easy to pack up and take to a party. Garnish with a basil sprig and serve surrounded with crackers, if you like.

PREP: 30 MINUTES PLUS OVERNIGHT TO CHILL   MAKES ABOUT 3 1/2 CUPS

1 ounce dried tomatoes (8 tomato halves)

3 packages (8 ounces each) cream cheese, softened

2 cups loosely packed fresh basil leaves

1/2 cup loosely packed fresh parsley leaves

6 tablespoons freshly grated Parmesan cheese

1/2 teaspoon salt

3/4 teaspoon ground black pepper

1 tablespoon tomato paste

1. Line 1-quart bowl with plastic wrap, allowing excess to extend over rim of bowl. In 1-quart saucepan, combine dried tomatoes and enough *water* to cover; heat to boiling. Remove from heat; let stand 10 minutes. Drain tomatoes and pat dry with paper towels; coarsely chop (you should have about 1/3 cup).

2. Meanwhile, in food processor with knife blade attached, puree 1 package cream cheese, basil, parsley, 1 tablespoon Parmesan, 1/4 teaspoon salt, and 1/4 teaspoon pepper until smooth. Spoon into prepared bowl and smooth top.

3. Wash food processor. In clean food processor, puree 1 package cream cheese, 4 tablespoons Parmesan, and 1/4 teaspoon pepper until smooth. Spoon white mixture evenly over basil mixture in bowl.

4. Combine remaining package cream cheese, dried tomatoes, tomato paste, remaining 1 tablespoon Parmesan, remaining 1/4 teaspoon salt, and 1/4 teaspoon pepper in food processor (no need to clean processor); puree until smooth. Spoon evenly over white mixture in bowl. Cover and refrigerate at least 8 hours or up to 2 days. To serve, unwrap and place on large plate.

Each tablespoon: About 36 calories, 2g protein, 1g carbohydrate, 3g total fat (0g saturated), 0g fiber, 9mg cholesterol, 59mg sodium.

Tapenade

Enjoy this flavorful olive spread on crisp toasted bread or crackers.

PREP: 20 MINUTES COOK: 3 MINUTES MAKES ABOUT 1¼ CUPS

2 garlic cloves, peeled
1 cup Gaeta or Kalamata olives,
   pitted
½ cup pimiento-stuffed olives

1 tablespoon olive oil
1 teaspoon fennel seeds
1 teaspoon freshly grated orange
   peel

1. In 1-quart saucepan, heat *2 cups water* to boiling over high heat. Add garlic and cook 3 minutes to blanch; drain.

2. In food processor with knife blade attached, combine Gaeta and pimiento-stuffed olives, oil, fennel seeds, orange peel, and garlic; process until finely chopped.

Each tablespoon: About 11 calories, 0g protein, 1g carbohydrate, 1g total fat (0g saturated), 0g fiber, 0mg cholesterol, 62mg sodium.

Caponata

Caponata makes a tasty side dish, relish, or contribution to an antipasto platter. Or spread it on toasted Italian bread for fabulous bruschetta.

PREP: 30 MINUTES PLUS COOLING   COOK: 40 MINUTES
MAKES ABOUT 5 CUPS

2 small eggplants (1 pound each), unpeeled, cut into 3/4-inch pieces
1/2 cup extravirgin olive oil
1/4 teaspoon salt
3 small red onions, thinly sliced
4 ripe medium tomatoes (11/2 pounds), peeled, seeded, and chopped
1 cup Mediterranean olives, such as Niçoise, picholine, or Kalamata, pitted and chopped

3 tablespoons capers, drained
3 tablespoons golden raisins
1/4 teaspoon coarsely ground black pepper
4 stalks celery with leaves, thinly sliced
1/3 cup red wine vinegar
2 teaspoons sugar
1/4 cup chopped fresh flat-leaf parsley

1. Preheat oven to 450°F. Spread eggplant in two 15 1/2" by 10 1/2" jelly-roll pans. Drizzle with 1/4 cup oil and sprinkle with salt; toss to coat. Roast eggplant 10 minutes; stir, then roast until browned, about 10 minutes longer.

2. Meanwhile, in 12-inch skillet, heat remaining 1/4 cup oil over medium heat until hot but not smoking. Add onions and cook, stirring, 10 minutes, or until very soft but not browned. Add tomatoes, olives, capers, raisins, and pepper; reduce heat to low and simmer, covered, 15 minutes.

3. Add eggplant and celery to skillet and cook over medium heat, stirring, until celery is just tender, 8 to 10 minutes. Stir in vinegar and sugar and cook 1 minute. Cool to room temperature, or cover and refrigerate up to overnight. To serve, sprinkle with parsley.

Each 1/4 cup: About 83 calories, 1g protein, 7g carbohydrate, 6g total fat (1g saturated), 2g fiber, 0mg cholesterol, 133mg sodium.

Pork Rillettes

Typically found in French bistros, rillettes is a spread made with delicately seasoned pork, slowly cooked until it is falling-apart tender. It was traditionally cooked in lard, seasoned, and pounded to a smooth paste. It will keep refrigerated up to 1 week. Serve as an hors d'oeuvre on crackers or toast or with a sliced baguette.

PREP: 5 MINUTES PLUS OVERNIGHT TO CHILL   COOK: 3 1/2 HOURS
MAKES 2 CUPS

3 pounds boneless pork shoulder
  blade roast (fresh pork butt), cut
  into 1/2-inch pieces
2 cups water
2 teaspoons salt
1 1/2 teaspoons coarsely ground
  black pepper

1/2 teaspoon dried thyme
1/8 teaspoon ground allspice
1 bay leaf
1 garlic clove, crushed with garlic
  press

1. In 5-quart Dutch oven, combine pork, water, salt, pepper, thyme, allspice, bay leaf, and garlic; heat to boiling over high heat. Reduce heat to low; cover and simmer, stirring occasionally, until meat is very tender and falls apart when tested with fork, about 2 1/2 hours.

2. When meat is done, uncover Dutch oven and reduce heat to low. Cook, stirring frequently, until liquid has evaporated. Discard bay leaf.

3. With two forks, shred meat. Spoon mixture into small jar or 2-cup covered crock; pack down well. Refrigerate overnight to allow flavors to blend. Let stand 1 hour at room temperature before serving.

Each tablespoon: About 115 calories, 10g protein, 0g carbohydrate, 8g total fat (3g saturated), 0g fiber, 37mg cholesterol, 29mg sodium.

Salmon Rillettes

Fresh and smoked salmon make a winning flavor combination. Serve with sliced French bread.

PREP: 30 MINUTES PLUS CHILLING   COOK: 8 MINUTES
MAKES ABOUT 2 1/2 CUPS

1 teaspoon salt
8 ounces skinless salmon fillet
1 large lemon
8 ounces smoked salmon, finely
    chopped
1/2 cup butter or margarine (1 stick),
    softened

2 tablespoons plus 1 teaspoon
    chopped fresh chives
1 teaspoon Dijon mustard
1 teaspoon capers, drained and
    chopped
1/8 teaspoon coarsely ground black
    pepper

1. Poach salmon: In 10-inch skillet, heat *4 cups water* and salt to boiling over high heat. Add salmon fillet; heat to boiling. Reduce heat to low; cover and simmer until salmon is opaque throughout, 8 to 10 minutes. With wide spatula, carefully lift salmon from water; drain salmon (still resting on spatula) on paper towels. Transfer salmon to medium bowl; cool slightly.

2. Meanwhile, from lemon, grate 1 teaspoon peel and squeeze 2 tablespoons juice.

3. With wooden spoon, stir and mash poached salmon almost to smooth paste. Add smoked salmon, butter, 2 tablespoons chives, mustard, capers, lemon peel and juice, and pepper; blend thoroughly.

4. Spoon salmon mixture into crock or serving bowl. Cover and refrigerate for at least 2 hours or up to overnight. Before serving, let stand 30 minutes at room temperature, or until soft enough to spread. Sprinkle with remaining 1 teaspoon chives.

Each tablespoon: About 35 calories, 2g protein, 0g carbohydrate, 3g total fat (1g saturated), 0g fiber, 5mg cholesterol, 90mg sodium.

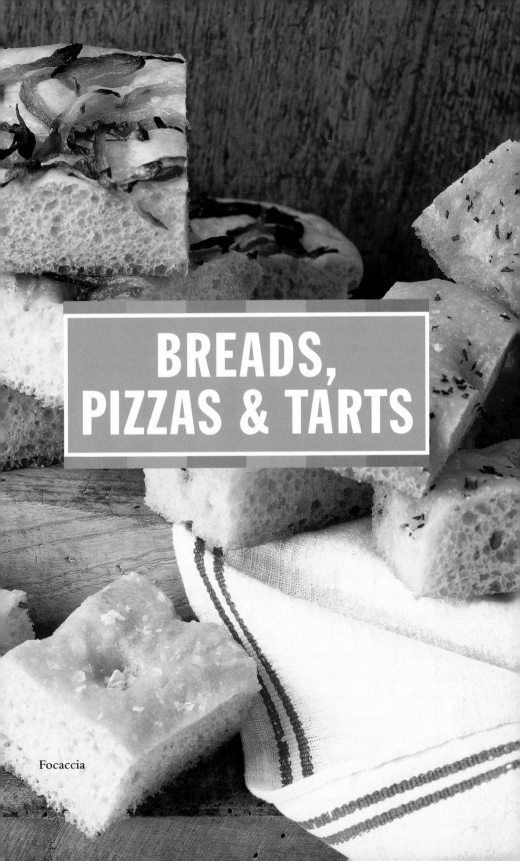

BREADS, PIZZAS & TARTS

Focaccia

Rustic Tomato Tart

If you can't find yellow tomatoes, all reds are fine.

PREP: 35 MINUTES PLUS CHILLING   BAKE/BROIL: 31 MINUTES
MAKES 12 FIRST-COURSE SERVINGS

CRUST
1 1/2 cups all-purpose flour
1/2 teaspoon salt
4 tablespoons cold butter or
    margarine, cut into pieces
1/4 cup vegetable shortening
3 to 4 tablespoons ice water

FILLING
1 tablespoon olive oil
3 medium onions (5 ounces each),
    thinly sliced

1/2 teaspoon salt
1/4 cup Kalamata olives
1 package (3 1/2 ounces) mild goat
    cheese, crumbled
1 ripe medium yellow tomato
    (8 ounces), cut into 1/4-inch-thick
    slices
2 ripe medium red tomatoes
    (8 ounces each), cut into 1/4-inch-
    thick slices
1/2 teaspoon coarsely ground black
    pepper

1. Preheat oven to 425°F. Prepare crust: In large bowl, combine flour and salt. With pastry blender or two knives used scissor-fashion, cut in butter and shortening until mixture resembles coarse crumbs.

2. Sprinkle in ice water, 1 tablespoon at a time, mixing lightly with fork after each addition until dough is just moist enough to hold together.

3. Shape dough into disk; wrap in plastic wrap. Refrigerate 30 minutes or up to overnight. (If chilled overnight, let stand 30 minutes at room temperature before rolling out.)

4. On lightly floured surface, with floured rolling pin, roll dough into a 14-inch round. Ease dough into 11" tart pan with removable bottom. Fold overhang in and press against side of pan so it extends 1/8 inch above rim. Refrigerate or freeze until firm, 10 to 15 minutes.

5. Line tart shell with foil; fill with pie weights or dried beans. Bake 20 minutes. Remove foil with weights. Bake until golden, 5 to 10 minutes longer. If shell puffs up during baking, gently press it down with back of spoon.

6. Meanwhile prepare filling: In nonstick 12-inch skillet, heat oil over medium heat. Add onions and 1/4 teaspoon salt; cook, stirring frequently, until onions are tender and golden, about 20 minutes. Reserve 3 or 4 olives for garnish. Pit and slice remaining olives.

7. Turn oven control to broil. Spoon onions over bottom of tart shell and crumble half of goat cheese on top. Arrange yellow and red tomatoes, alternating colors, in concentric circles over onion-cheese mixture. Sprinkle with remaining 1/4 teaspoon salt and pepper. Crumble remaining goat cheese on top of tart.

8. Place tart on rack in broiling pan. Place pan about 7 inches from heat source. Broil until cheese has melted and tomatoes are heated through, 6 to 8 minutes. Sprinkle with whole and sliced olives.

Each serving: About 195 calories, 4g protein, 19g carbohydrate, 12g total fat (4g saturated), 1g fiber, 4mg cholesterol, 308mg sodium.

Rustic Tomato Tart

Caramelized Onion and Goat Cheese Tart

A rich, golden pastry crust is the perfect foil for our cheese-topped filling. If you can't find mild goat cheese, such as Montrachet, use one-third cup freshly grated Parmesan instead. If you like, you can prepare and bake the crust and prepare the vinaigrette up to three days ahead. The crust can be stored at room temperature, covered with foil; the vinaigrette should be refrigerated. Caramelize the onions up to two days ahead, then place in a zip-tight plastic bag and refrigerate.

PREP: 1 HOUR 15 MINUTES BAKE: 1 HOUR
MAKES 10 FIRST-COURSE SERVINGS

CRUST
- 1 1/2 cups all-purpose flour
- 1/2 teaspoon salt
- 4 tablespoons cold butter or margarine, cut into pieces
- 1/4 cup vegetable shortening
- 3 to 4 tablespoons ice water

FILLING
- 1 tablespoon butter or margarine
- 1 tablespoon olive oil
- 2 jumbo onions (1 pound each), each cut lengthwise in half, then cut crosswise into thin slices
- 1/2 teaspoon salt
- 1/4 teaspoon coarsely ground black pepper
- 2 tablespoons water
- 3 large eggs
- 1 cup milk
- 2/3 cup half-and-half or light cream
- 1 package (3 1/2 ounces) mild goat cheese, crumbled

SALAD
- 1 tablespoon olive oil
- 2 teaspoons seasoned rice vinegar
- 2 teaspoons balsamic vinegar
- 1/4 teaspoon Dijon mustard
- 1/8 teaspoon salt
- 1/8 teaspoon coarsely ground black pepper
- 6 ounces mixed baby greens (about 10 cups)
- 1/4 cup loosely packed fresh parsley leaves, chopped

1. Preheat oven to 425°F. Prepare crust: In large bowl, combine flour and salt. With pastry blender or two knives used scissor-fashion, cut in butter and shortening until mixture resembles coarse crumbs.

2. Sprinkle in ice water, 1 tablespoon at a time, mixing lightly with fork after each addition until dough is just moist enough to hold together.

3. On lightly floured surface, with floured rolling pin, roll dough into a 14-inch round. Ease dough into 11" tart pan with removable bottom. Fold overhang in and press against side of pan so it extends 1/8 inch above rim. With fork, prick dough at 1-inch intervals to prevent puffing and shrinking during baking. Refrigerate or freeze until firm, 10 to 15 minutes.

4. Line tart shell with foil and fill with pie weights or dried beans. Bake 15 minutes; remove foil with weights. Bake until golden about 15 minutes longer. If shell puffs up during baking, gently press it down with back of spoon. Remove tart shell from oven; cool on wire rack.

5. Meanwhile, prepare filling: Turn oven control to 400°F. In nonstick 12-inch skillet, melt butter with oil over medium heat. Add onions, salt, and pepper; cook, stirring occasionally, until onions are tender and golden, 25 to 30 minutes; stir in water during last minute of cooking time.

6. In medium bowl, with wire whisk, mix eggs, milk, and half-and-half until blended.

7. Spread onions over bottom of tart shell; pour egg mixture over. Bake until filling is set and lightly browned, 25 to 30 minutes. Crumble goat cheese on top of tart; bake 3 minutes longer. Transfer tart to wire rack; let stand 10 minutes to serve hot. Or, cool and serve at room temperature.

8. Meanwhile, prepare salad: In small bowl, with wire whisk, mix oil, rice and balsamic vinegars, mustard, salt, and pepper until blended.

9. To serve, in large bowl, toss greens with vinaigrette. Sprinkle tart with parsley; cut into 10 wedges. Serve each wedge with some salad.

Each serving: About 249 calories, 7g protein, 20g carbohydrate, 15g total fat (8g saturated), 1g fiber, 94mg cholesterol, 157mg sodium.

Flatbread with Salad

Flatbread with Salad

Try this salad "pizza" as an alternative to the usual tomato-and-cheese kind. It's especially good because it starts with our crusty Grilled Flatbread. The flatbread dough can be prepared up to twenty-four hours ahead. Prepare the dough, but rather than let it rise at room temperature, transfer it to a greased bowl, cover loosely with greased plastic wrap, and refrigerate up to twenty-four hours. Bring the dough to room temperature before proceeding with the recipe.

PREP: 35 MINUTES PLUS DOUGH RISING AND RESTING
GRILL: 4 MINUTES PER FLATBREAD
MAKES 8 FIRST-COURSE SERVINGS

Grilled Flatbread (page 82)
2 tablespoons extravirgin olive oil
2 tablespoons red wine vinegar
1 teaspoon sugar
1 teaspoon Dijon mustard
1/4 teaspoon salt
1/8 teaspoon ground black pepper

6 cups torn salad greens, such as radicchio, endive, and arugula
2 ripe medium tomatoes, cut into 1/2-inch pieces
1 small cucumber, peeled and cut into 1/2-inch pieces

1. Prepare Grilled Flatbread through step 5 as directed.
2. About 10 minutes before grilling flatbread, prepare salad topping: In large bowl, with wire whisk, mix oil, vinegar, sugar, mustard, salt, and pepper until blended.
3. Add salad greens, tomatoes, and cucumber to dressing in bowl; toss to coat well. Set aside.
4. Grill flatbreads as directed in step 6 of flatbread recipe.
5. To serve, top each flatbread with about 2 cups salad. Cut each round into 4 wedges.

Each serving: About 310 calories, 8g protein, 53g carbohydrate, 7g total fat (1g saturated), 3g fiber, 0mg cholesterol, 625mg sodium.

Grilled Flatbread

Cooking this bread on the grill gives it a unique look and imparts a rustic flavor. Serve with herb-infused olive oil and fresh herbs.

PREP: 15 MINUTES PLUS RISING   GRILL: 5 MINUTES PER FLATBREAD
MAKES 16 APPETIZERS

1¼ cups warm water (105° to 115°F)	about 4 cups all-purpose flour
1 package active dry yeast	about 3 tablespoons olive oil
1 teaspoon sugar	2 teaspoons salt

1. In large bowl, combine ¼ cup water, yeast, and sugar; stir to dissolve. Let stand until foamy, about 5 minutes. With wooden spoon, stir in 1½ cups flour, remaining 1 cup warm water, 2 tablespoons oil, and salt until combined. Gradually stir in 2 cups flour. With floured hand, knead mixture in bowl to combine well.

2. Turn dough onto lightly floured surface; knead until smooth and elastic, about 10 minutes, working in enough of remaining ½ cup flour just to keep dough from sticking.

3. Shape dough into ball; place in greased large bowl, turning dough to grease top. Cover bowl with greased plastic wrap and let rise in a warm place (80° to 85°F) until doubled in volume, about 1 hour. (After dough has risen, if not using dough right away, punch down and leave in bowl, covered loosely with greased plastic wrap. Refrigerate up to 24 hours.)

4. Grease 2 large cookie sheets. Punch down dough. Turn dough onto lightly floured surface. Cover and let rest 15 minutes.

5. Prepare grill. Cut dough into 4 equal pieces: shape each piece into ball. With floured rolling pin, roll 1 dough ball at a time into an ⅛-inch-thick round that is about 12 inches in diameter. Place dough rounds on prepared cookie sheets; lightly brush dough with some remaining oil.

6. With hands, place 1 round at a time, greased side down, on grill over medium heat. Grill until grill marks appear on underside and dough stiffens (dough may puff slightly), 2 to 3 minutes. Brush top with some oil. With tongs, turn bread; grill until marks appear on underside and bread is cooked through, 2 to 3 minutes longer. Cut each flatbread into 4 wedges and serve warm.

Each appetizer: About 155 calories, 5g protein, 26g carbohydrate, 4g total fat (0g saturated), 2g fiber, 0mg cholesterol, 294mg sodium.

Flatbread with Zahtar

Top grilled flatbread with this popular Middle Eastern spread.

PREP: 30 MINUTES PLUS DOUGH RISING AND RESTING
GRILL: 4 MINUTES PER FLATBREAD MAKES 12 APPETIZERS

Grilled Flatbread (page 82)
2 large lemons
1/2 cup sesame seeds, toasted
1/3 cup olive oil
3 tablespoons chopped fresh parsley

1 garlic clove, crushed with garlic
 press
2 teaspoons dried thyme
1/2 teaspoon salt
pinch ground red pepper (cayenne)

1. Prepare Grilled Flatbread as directed through Step 4.

2. While dough is resting, prepare zahtar topping: From lemons, grate 1 tablespoon peel and squeeze 2 tablespoons juice. In small bowl, stir lemon peel and juice, sesame seeds, oil, parsley, garlic, thyme, salt, and ground red pepper until well combined.

3. Roll dough out as directed in Step 5 of flatbread recipe.

4. Grill dough rounds as directed in Step 6 of flatbread recipe, but after turning each round over, do not brush with oil. With small metal spatula or spoon, spread scant 1/4 cup zahtar mixture on top of each flatbread. Grill until grill marks appear on underside and bread is cooked through, 2 to 3 minutes longer. Repeat with remaining dough and zahtar mixture.

5. To serve, cut each flatbread into 6 wedges.

Each appetizer: About 265 calories, 6g protein, 34g carbohydrate, 12g total fat (2g saturated), 1g fiber, 0mg cholesterol, 445mg sodium.

Pita-Crisp Appetizers

If you like, assemble the appetizers up to one hour before serving; place on platters or in jelly-roll pans, and cover with plastic wrap or foil. For a real head start, the pitas can be toasted and stored at room temperature in zip-tight plastic bags for up to two weeks.

PREP: 20 MINUTES   BAKE/COOK: 26 MINUTES   MAKES 64 APPETIZERS

1 package (8 ounces) mini (4-inch) pitas (per topping)
Sweet Tomato Topping (below)

crumbled mild goat cheese (optional)
fresh thyme leaves (optional)

1. Preheat oven to 425°F. With knife, cut each pita horizontally in half. Cut each round into 4 wedges. Place wedges, smooth side down, on 2 large cookie sheets. Bake wedges until golden brown, 6 to 8 minutes, rotating cookie sheets between upper and lower oven racks halfway through baking. Transfer pita crisps to wire racks to cool completely.

2. Prepare Sweet Tomato Topping; cover and refrigerate until ready to use.

3. To serve, spoon about 1 rounded teaspoon topping on each pita crisp. If you like, top tomato mixture with some goat cheese and thyme leaves.

Each pita crisp with topping: About 20 calories, 1g protein, 4g carbohydrate, 1g total fat (0g saturated), 0g fiber, 0mg cholesterol, 80mg sodium.

Sweet Tomato Topping

Drain liquid from **2 cans (28 ounces each) whole tomatoes in juice;** coarsely chop tomatoes. In 4-quart saucepan, heat **2 tablespoons olive oil** over medium heat until hot. Add **1 medium onion, finely chopped,** and cook, stirring occasionally, until tender and golden, about 10 minutes. Stir in tomatoes, **1/2 cup red wine vinegar, 1/3 cup packed brown sugar, 1 teaspoon salt,** and **1/4 teaspoon coarsely ground black pepper;** heat to boiling over high heat. Cook over high heat, stirring occasionally, until liquid has evaporated and mixture thickens, about 25 minutes. Transfer to bowl to cool. Cover and refrigerate up to 2 days. Makes about 2 3/4 cups.

Pistachio-Sesame Pita Crisps

Delicious on their own or with our Moroccan Dip (page 42).

PREP: 25 MINUTES PLUS COOLING BAKE: 6 MINUTES
MAKES 64 CRISPS

1/2 cup pistachios (about 4 ounces unshelled), shells removed
1/4 cup sesame seeds
1/4 teaspoon salt

1 package (8 ounces) mini pitas (4 inches in diameter), each cut horizontally in half
6 tablespoons olive oil

1. Preheat oven to 425°F. In food processor with knife blade attached, combine pistachios, sesame seeds, and salt; process until finely ground. Transfer to waxed paper.
2. Cut each pita-bread round into 4 wedges. Brush rough sides of pita wedges with oil; lightly press wedges, oil side down, into pistachio mixture (about 1/2 teaspoon pistachio mixture for each wedge).
3. Place pita wedges, pistachio side up, on 2 large cookie sheets. Bake until golden brown, 6 to 8 minutes, rotating cookie sheets between upper and lower oven racks halfway through baking. Transfer crisps to wire racks to cool completely. Store in airtight container up to 2 weeks.

Each crisp: About 30 calories, 1g protein, 2g carbohydrate, 2g total fat (0g saturated), 0g fiber, 0mg cholesterol, 30mg sodium.

Quick and Easy Antipasti

Antipasti (appetizers that arrive "before the pasta") follow the Italian philosophy of cooking: uncomplicated food made with the freshest, highest-quality ingredients, lovingly prepared and simply presented. Eight classics to try:

- Cut a thin slice off the top (stem end) of a pint of cherry tomatoes. Scoop out and discard the seeds using a melon baller or teaspoon. Fill with flaked Italian tuna packed in olive oil or with a mixture of softened goat cheese, chopped basil, extravirgin olive oil, salt, and ground black pepper.
- Spread ricotta cheese over thin slices of Italian bread; transfer to cookie sheet, drizzle with extravirgin olive oil, and sprinkle with salt and ground black pepper. Bake in a preheated 450°F oven about ten minutes or until the cheese bubbles.
- Fill pitted dates with chunks of Parmesan or Pecorino Romano cheese.
- Wrap thinly sliced smoked salmon around crisp breadsticks.
- Prepare a tray of assorted cured meats, such as salami, mortadella, soppressata, pancetta, prosciutto, coppa, and bresaola.
- Marinate small whole mushrooms, jarred roasted red peppers, canned quartered artichoke hearts, or small fresh mozzarella balls (bocconcini) in a mixture of extravirgin olive oil, wine vinegar, sliced fresh basil, crushed red pepper, and salt.
- Serve small bowls of assorted pickled vegetables such as pearl onions, sweet or sour pickles, carrots, cauliflower, pepperoncini, and olives.
- Thickly slice large balls of fresh mozzarella and ripe tomatoes. Arrange on a platter, overlapping in concentric circles, alternating the tomatoes and cheese, and tucking in a basil leaf between each slice. Finish the dish by drizzling with high-quality extravirgin olive oil and sprinkling with coarse sea salt and freshly ground black pepper.

Bruschetta with Tomatoes, Basil, and Olives

The classic Mediterranean combination of herbs, tomatoes, and olives on toasted Italian (or French) bread makes a nice nibble when serving drinks by the pool or on the deck.

PREP: 20 MINUTES BROIL: 2 MINUTES MAKES ABOUT 16 BRUSCHETTA

1 loaf (8 ounces) Italian bread, cut on diagonal into 1/2-inch-thick slices
1 garlic clove, peeled and cut in half
8 ripe small tomatoes (about 1 1/2 pounds) chopped
1/4 cup Kalamata olives, pitted and chopped
1/4 cup loosely packed fresh basil leaves, chopped
1/4 cup loosely packed fresh parsley leaves, chopped
3 tablespoons extravirgin olive oil
1/4 teaspoon salt
1/8 teaspoon ground black pepper

1. Preheat broiler. Place bread slices in 15 1/2" by 10 1/2" jelly-roll pan. Place pan in broiler at closest position to heat source; broil bread until lightly toasted, about 1 minute on each side. Rub one side of each toast slice with cut side of garlic.

2. In medium bowl, gently toss tomatoes, olives, basil, parsley, oil, salt, and pepper until combined.

3. To serve, spoon tomato mixture on garlic-rubbed side of toast slices.

Each bruschetta: About 70 calories, 1g protein, 9g carbohydrate, 4g total fat (1g saturated), 1g fiber, 0mg cholesterol, 145mg sodium.

Lemony White Bean Bruschetta

PREP: 20 MINUTES   GRILL: 2 MINUTES   MAKES 16 BRUSCHETTA

1 lemon
1 can (15 to 19 ounces) white kidney
  beans (cannellini), rinsed and
  drained
1 tablespoon plus 1 teaspoon
  chopped fresh parsley leaves
1 tablespoon olive oil

1/4 teaspoon salt
1/8 teaspoon coarsely ground pepper
1 loaf (8 ounces) Italian bread, cut
  on diagonal into 1/2-inch-thick
  slices
2 garlic cloves, each cut in half

1. Prepare grill.

2. Meanwhile, from lemon, grate 1/2 teaspoon peel and squeeze 1 tablespoon juice. In medium bowl, with fork, lightly mash beans with 1 tablespoon parsley, lemon peel and juice, oil, salt, and pepper.

3. Place bread slices on grill rack over medium heat and grill bread slices until lightly toasted, about 1 minute per side. Rub one side of each toast slice with cut side of garlic.

4. To serve, spoon bean mixture on garlic-rubbed side of toast and sprinkle with remaining 1 teaspoon parsley.

Each bruschetta: About 70 calories, 3g protein, 12g carbohydrate, 2g total fat (1g saturated), 2g fiber, 0mg cholesterol, 155mg sodium.

Lemony White Bean Bruschetta

Tomato and Ricotta Salata Bruschetta

Bruschetta is toasted Italian bread that is rubbed with garlic and drizzled with olive oil. It's often topped with savory ingredients to make a simple appetizer. Here we use ripe tomatoes and ricotta salata, a lightly salted pressed sheep's milk cheese. Ricotta salata can be found at Italian markets and specialty food stores.

PREP: 25 MINUTES   MAKES: 16 BRUSCHETTA

1 loaf (8 ounces) Italian bread, cut on diagonal into 1/2-inch-thick slices
8 garlic cloves, each cut in half
1 pound ripe plum tomatoes (6 medium), seeded and cut into 1/2-inch pieces
1 tablespoon finely chopped red onion
1 tablespoon chopped fresh basil
4 ounces ricotta salata, feta, or goat cheese, cut into 1/2-inch pieces
2 tablespoons extravirgin olive oil
2 teaspoons balsamic vinegar
1/4 teaspoon salt
1/4 teaspoon coarsely ground black pepper

1. Preheat oven to 400°F. Place bread slices on cookie sheet and bake until lightly toasted, about 5 minutes. Rub one side of each toast slice with cut side of garlic.
2. Meanwhile, in bowl, gently toss tomatoes, onion, basil, ricotta salata, oil, vinegar, salt, and pepper until combined.
3. To serve, spoon tomato mixture on garlic-rubbed side of toast slices.

Each bruschetta: About 79 calories, 2g protein, 9g carbohydrate, 4g total fat (1g saturated), 1g fiber, 6mg cholesterol, 236mg sodium.

Tuscan White Bean Bruschetta

Prepare toast as directed. Instead of preparing tomato-cheese topping, in bowl, with fork, lightly mash **1 can (15 1/2 to 19 ounces) white kidney beans (cannellini)**, rinsed and drained, with **1 tablespoon fresh lemon juice**. Stir in **1 tablespoon olive oil, 2 teaspoons chopped** fresh parsley, **1 teaspoon finely chopped fresh sage**, **1/4 teaspoon salt**, and **1/8 teaspoon coarsely ground black pepper**. To serve, spoon mixture over garlic-rubbed side of toast slices. Sprinkle with **1 teaspoon chopped fresh parsley**. Makes 16 bruschetta.

Each bruschetta: About 33 calories, 2g protein, 4g carbohydrate, 1g total fat (0g saturated), 7g fiber, 0mg cholesterol, 77mg sodium.

Tomato and Ricotta Salata Bruschetta & Tuscan White Bean Bruschetta

Pear Chutney and Goat-Cheese Bruschetta

PREP: 30 MINUTES PLUS COOLING   COOK: 25 MINUTES
MAKES 16 BRUSCHETTA

1 loaf (8 ounces) Italian bread, cut on diagonal into 1/2-inch-thick slices (16 slices)
4 large firm ripe pears, such as Bosc or Anjou (about 2 pounds), peeled, cored, and cut into 1/2-inch pieces
1/3 cup packed brown sugar
1/3 cup dark raisins, chopped
1/3 cup cider vinegar

2 teaspoons grated, peeled fresh ginger
1/2 teaspoon Chinese five-spice powder
1/4 teaspoon salt
1 log (10 ounces) mild goat cheese, softened
fresh flat-leaf parsley leaves

1. Preheat oven to 350°F. Place bread slices on 2 cookie sheets and bake until crusty and dry, about 10 minutes, turning slices over once. Transfer bread to wire racks to cool.

2. Meanwhile, prepare pear chutney: In nonstick 12-inch skillet, combine pears, brown sugar, raisins, vinegar, ginger, five-spice powder, and salt. Cook over medium heat until liquid has evaporated and sugar caramelizes, 25 to 30 minutes, stirring frequently during last 10 minutes of cooking. Mixture will become very thick and turn dark brown. Remove from heat and cool to room temperature. Can be prepared up to 1 week ahead and stored in refrigerator.

3. To serve, spread 1 rounded teaspoon goat cheese evenly on each toast slice. Top each with 1 scant tablespoon pear chutney and a parsley leaf.

Each bruschetta: About 70 calories, 3g protein, 11g carbohydrate, 2g total fat (1g saturated), 1g fiber, 4mg cholesterol, 95mg sodium.

Rosemary-Fennel Breadsticks

These breadsticks keep perfectly for up to two weeks in an airtight container. If you happen to have some fresh rosemary on hand, substitute two to three teaspoons for the dried. Just be sure it is chopped.

PREP: 40 MINUTES   BAKE: 20 MINUTES PER BATCH
MAKES 64 BREADSTICKS

about 4³/₄ cups all-purpose flour
2 packages quick-rise yeast
2¹/₂ teaspoons salt
2 teaspoons fennel seeds, crushed
1 teaspoon dried rosemary, crumbled

¹/₂ teaspoon coarsely ground black pepper
1¹/₃ cups very warm water (120° to 130°F)
¹/₂ cup olive oil

1. In large bowl, combine 2 cups flour, yeast, salt, fennel seeds, rosemary, and pepper. With wooden spoon, stir in very warm water; beat vigorously 1 minute. Stir in oil. Gradually stir in 2¹/₄ cups flour.

2. Turn dough onto lightly floured surface and knead until smooth and elastic, about 8 minutes, working in enough of remaining ¹/₂ cup flour just to keep dough from sticking. Cover dough loosely with plastic wrap; let rest 10 minutes.

3. Meanwhile, preheat oven to 375°F. Grease 2 large cookie sheets. Divide dough in half. Cover one dough half; cut remaining dough half into 32 equal pieces. Shape each piece into 12-inch-long rope. Place ropes 1 inch apart on prepared cookie sheets.

4. Bake breadsticks until golden and crisp, about 20 minutes, rotating cookie sheets between upper and lower oven racks halfway through baking. Transfer to wire racks to cool. Repeat with remaining dough.

Each breadstick: About 50 calories, 1g protein, 7g carbohydrate, 2g total fat (0g saturated), 0g fiber, 0mg cholesterol, 85mg sodium.

Lemon-Pepper Crisps

These paper-thin flatbreads are great on their own, with your favorite dip, or with soup.

PREP: 50 MINUTES PLUS COOLING   BAKE: 15 MINUTES PER BATCH
MAKES 36 CRISPS

2 1/4 cups all-purpose flour
2 1/4 teaspoons kosher salt
1 1/2 teaspoons baking powder
1/4 teaspoon coarsely ground black pepper
1 cup loosely packed fresh parsley leaves, finely chopped
1 tablespoon freshly grated lemon peel
3/4 cup water
2 tablespoons olive oil

1. In medium bowl, combine flour, 2 teaspoons kosher salt, baking powder, and pepper. Add parsley and lemon peel; stir until combined. Add water; with wooden spoon, stir until dough comes together in a ball. With hand, knead dough in bowl until smooth, about 2 minutes. Divide dough in half; cover each dough half with plastic wrap; let rest 10 minutes.

2. Preheat oven to 350°F. On lightly floured surface, with floured rolling pin, roll one dough half into paper-thin rectangle, about 18" by 12" (don't worry if edges are irregular). With pizza wheel or sharp knife, cut dough lengthwise in half to form two rectangles. Cut each rectangle crosswise into 2-inch-wide strips.

3. Place strips about 1 inch apart on 2 ungreased large cookie sheets (it's okay if dough stretches a little); let rest 10 minutes. With pastry brush, brush strips lightly with 1 tablespoon oil; sprinkle with remaining 1/4 teaspoon salt.

4. Bake strips until lightly browned, 15 to 18 minutes, rotating cookie sheets between upper and lower oven racks halfway through baking. Immediately transfer crisps to wire racks to cool.

5. Repeat with remaining dough, oil, and salt. Store crisps in airtight container up to 2 weeks.

Each crisp: About 35 calories, 1g protein, 6g carbohydrate, 1g total fat (0g saturated), 0g fiber, 0mg cholesterol, 90mg sodium.

Phyllo Sticks

The unbaked phyllo sticks can be refrigerated or frozen. Place sticks on cookie sheets, cover with foil, and refrigerate up to four hours. Remove foil and bake as directed. Up to one month ahead, place sticks in a freezer-safe container with waxed paper between layers. Place frozen sticks on cookie sheets and bake in preheated 425°F oven, allowing eight to ten minutes per batch.

PREP: 25 MINUTES PLUS COOLING BAKE: 5 MINUTES PER BATCH
MAKES 48 PHYLLO STICKS

1 cup grated Romano cheese
1 tablespoon coarsely ground black
  pepper

12 sheets (16" by 12" each) fresh or
  frozen (thawed) phyllo
5 tablespoons butter or margarine,
  melted

1. Prepare filling: In cup, combine Romano and pepper.
2. On waxed paper, place 1 phyllo sheet and brush with some melted butter. Cover remaining phyllo with plastic wrap to prevent it from drying out. Sprinkle 1 rounded tablespoon filling over phyllo sheet.
3. Preheat oven to 425°F. Fold sheet crosswise in half. Starting from long open side, roll phyllo up tightly, jelly-roll fashion, toward folded side. Cut roll crosswise into 4 sticks. Place sticks 1 inch apart, seam side down, on large cookie sheet. Brush with melted butter. Repeat with remaining phyllo sheets and filling.
4. Bake sticks until golden brown, 5 to 7 minutes. Serve hot or at room temperature.

Each Romano & Pepper Stick: About 35 calories, 1g protein, 3g carbohydrate, 2g total fat (1g saturated), 0g fiber, 5mg cholesterol, 66mg sodium.

Sesame & Poppy Seed Phyllo Sticks

Prepare phyllo sticks as directed, but instead of Romano and Pepper filling, in cup, stir together **1/3 cup sesame seeds, 1/3 cup poppy seeds,** and **1/2 teaspoon salt.** In step 2, sprinkle 1 tablespoon seed mixture over each phyllo sheet. Makes 4 dozen.

Each Sesame & Poppy Seed Stick: About 35 calories, 1g protein, 3g carbohydrate, 2g total fat (1g saturated), 0g fiber, 3mg cholesterol, 37mg sodium.

Caraway Twists

Flavorful caraway seeds and crunchy kosher salt is a classic way to flavor up rolls and other yeast-type breads. If you prefer, however, you can substitute another favorite seed for the caraway.

PREP: 30 MINUTES PLUS RISING   BAKE: 16 MINUTES   MAKES 32 TWISTS

2 cups warm water (105° to 115°F)	about 4 cups all-purpose flour
1 package active dry yeast	1 tablespoon baking soda
1 teaspoon sugar	1 tablespoon kosher salt or coarse
1 teaspoon caraway seeds, crushed	sea salt
1 teaspoon table salt	

1. In large bowl, combine 1 1/2 cups warm water, yeast, and sugar; stir to dissolve. Let stand until foamy, about 5 minutes. Add caraway seeds, table salt, and 2 cups flour. Beat well with wooden spoon. Gradually stir in 1 1/2 cups flour to make soft dough.

2. Turn dough onto lightly floured surface; knead until smooth and elastic, 6 to 8 minutes, working in enough of remaining 1/2 cup flour just to keep dough from sticking.

3. Shape dough into ball; place in greased large bowl, turning dough over to grease top. Cover bowl with plastic wrap and let rise in warm place (80° to 85°F) until doubled in volume, about 30 minutes.

4. Preheat oven to 400°F. Grease 2 large cookie sheets. In small bowl, with wire whisk, whisk baking soda with remaining 1/2 cup warm water until soda dissolves.

5. Punch down dough. Turn dough onto lightly floured surface and cut into quarters. Working with 1 dough piece at a time (keep remaining dough covered with a clean kitchen towel), cut dough into 8 equal pieces. Shape each piece into 5" by 1" rope.

6. Dip ropes in baking soda mixture to coat. Place ropes 1 inch apart on prepared cookie sheets, twisting once to form a spiral and pressing ends against cookie sheet to prevent twists from uncurling. Repeat with remaining dough.

7. Sprinkle twists with kosher salt. Bake until browned, 16 to 18 minutes, rotating sheets between upper and lower oven racks halfway through baking. Transfer twists to wire racks to cool. Serve warm or at room temperature.

Each twist: About 60 calories, 2g protein, 12g carbohydrate, 0g total fat, 1g fiber, 0mg cholesterol, 270mg sodium.

Spicy Dallas Cheese Straws

Spicy Dallas Cheese Straws

Have an authentic Texas-style party and bring out lots of these boldly flavored and crispy cheese straws. Pile them onto a platter or place in a festive vase and use as a centerpiece.

PREP: 30 MINUTES BAKE: 20 MINUTES PER BATCH
MAKES ABOUT 48 CHEESE STRAWS

1 tablespoon paprika	1 package (17 1/4 ounces) frozen
1/2 teaspoon dried thyme	puff-pastry sheets, thawed
1/4 to 1/2 teaspoon ground red pepper	1 large egg white, lightly beaten
(cayenne)	8 ounces sharp Cheddar Cheese,
1/4 teaspoon salt	shredded (2 cups)

1. Preheat oven to 375°F. Grease 2 large cookie sheets. In small bowl, combine paprika, thyme, ground red pepper, and salt.

2. Unfold 1 puff-pastry sheet. On lightly floured surface, with floured rolling pin, roll pastry into 14-inch square. Lightly brush with egg white. Sprinkle half of paprika mixture on pastry. Sprinkle half of Cheddar on half of pastry. Fold pastry over to cover cheese, forming a rectangle. With rolling pin, lightly roll over pastry to seal layers together. With pizza wheel or knife, cut pastry crosswise into 1/2-inch-wide strips.

3. Place strips 1/2 inch apart on prepared cookie sheets, twisting each strip twice to form spiral and pressing ends against cookie sheet to prevent strips from uncurling. Bake cheese straws until golden, 20 to 22 minutes. With spatula, carefully transfer to wire racks to cool.

4. Repeat with remaining puff-pastry sheet, egg white, paprika mixture, and cheese. Store in airtight container up to 1 week.

Each cheese straw: About 75 calories, 2g protein, 5g carbohydrate, 6g total fat (2g saturated), 0g fiber, 9mg cholesterol, 65mg sodium.

Cheddar Straws

Cheese straws remain one of the most popular nibbles to enjoy with wine or other party drinks. We like the flavor of sharp Cheddar here, but extrasharp or even mild cheese can be used instead.

PREP: 1 HOUR PLUS FREEZING AND COOLING   BAKE: 15 MINUTES PER BATCH
MAKES 72 CHEESE STRAWS

2 cups all-purpose flour	1/2 cup ice water
1/2 teaspoon salt	1 large egg white, beaten
1 cup butter or margarine (2 sticks)	1 tablespoon sesame seeds
8 ounces sharp Cheddar cheese, shredded (2 cups)	1 tablespoon poppy seeds

1. In large bowl, combine flour and salt. With pastry blender or two knives used scissor-fashion, cut in butter until mixture resembles coarse crumbs. Stir in Cheddar and water just until mixture forms a soft dough and leaves side of bowl. On lightly floured surface, with floured hands, pat dough into 6-inch square. Wrap dough square in plastic wrap and freeze 30 minutes for easier handling.

2. On lightly floured surface, with floured rolling pin, roll chilled dough into 18" by 8" rectangle. Starting from an 8" side, fold dough over into middle; then fold opposite side over into middle (like folding a letter) to make 6" by 8" rectangle.

3. Repeat rolling and folding as directed in step 2. Wrap dough in plastic wrap and freeze 30 minutes.

4. Preheat oven to 375°F. Line 2 large cookie sheets with parchment paper.

5. Remove dough from freezer; roll and fold as directed in step 2. Roll dough into 18" by 12" rectangle; cut lengthwise in half. Cut each half crosswise into thirty-six 6" by 1/2" strips. Place strips 1/2" apart on prepared cookie sheets, twisting each strip twice and pressing ends against cookie sheets to prevent strips from uncurling.

6. Brush strips with egg white, then lightly sprinkle with sesame seeds and poppy seeds. Bake until golden, 15 minutes. Transfer to wire racks to cool. Store in airtight container at room temperature up to 1 week or in freezer up to 3 months.

Each straw: About 50 calories, 1g protein, 3g carbohydrate, 4g total fat (2g saturated), 0g fiber, 10mg cholesterol, 39mg sodium.

Olive Twists

Olive paste can be found in the Italian or gourmet section of many large supermarkets.

PREP: 30 MINUTES BAKE: 12 MINUTES MAKES ABOUT 56 TWISTS

1 package (8 ounces) feta cheese,
   well drained and crumbled
$1/3$ cup chopped fresh parsley
$1/3$ cup olive paste or $1/2$ cup
   Kalamata olives, pitted and pureed
   with 1 tablespoon olive oil

2 large egg whites
1 package ($17 1/4$ ounces) frozen
   puff-pastry sheets, thawed

1. Preheat oven to 400°F. Grease large cookie sheet. In small bowl, with fork, mix feta cheese, parsley, olive paste, and egg whites until thoroughly blended.

2. On lightly floured surface, unfold 1 puff-pastry sheet; keep other sheet refrigerated. Using floured rolling pin, roll pastry into 16" by 14" rectangle. Cut pastry crosswise in half. Spread half of olive mixture evenly over 1 pastry half; top with remaining pastry half. Using rolling pin, lightly roll over pastry to seal layers together.

3. With large chef's knife, cut pastry rectangle crosswise into $1/2$-inch-wide strips, taking care not to tear pastry. Twist each strip 3 to 4 times to form spiral, then place about 1 inch apart on prepared cookie sheet.

4. Bake strips, until puffed and lightly browned, 12 to 15 minutes. With wide spatula, transfer sticks to wire rack to cool. Repeat with remaining pastry sheet and olive mixture. Store in airtight container.

Each twist: About 55 calories, 1g protein, 5g carbohydrate, 4g total fat (1g saturated), 0g fiber, 4mg cholesterol, 80mg sodium.

Focaccia

This bread's wonderfully chewy texture and fine crumb are due to three risings. Sprinkle either two tablespoons chopped fresh sage or one tablespoon chopped fresh rosemary over the focaccia just before it is baked, if you wish.

PREP: 25 MINUTES PLUS RISING BAKE: 18 MINUTES MAKES 12 SERVINGS

1 1/2 cups warm water (105° to 115°F)
1 package active dry yeast
1 teaspoon sugar
5 tablespoons extravirgin olive oil

1 1/2 teaspoons table salt
3 3/4 cups all-purpose flour or 3 1/2 cups bread flour
1 teaspoon kosher or coarse sea salt

1. In large bowl, combine 1/2 cup warm water, yeast, and sugar; stir to dissolve. Let stand until foamy, about 5 minutes. Add remaining 1 cup warm water, 2 tablespoons oil, table salt, and flour; stir to combine.

2. Turn dough onto lightly floured surface and knead until smooth and elastic, about 7 minutes. Dough will be soft; do not add more flour.

3. Shape dough into ball; place in greased large bowl, turning dough to grease top. Cover bowl with plastic wrap and let stand in warm place (80° to 85°F) until doubled in volume, about 1 hour.

4. Lightly oil 15 1/2" by 10 1/2" jelly-roll pan. Punch dough down and pat into prepared pan. Cover with plastic wrap and let rise in warm place until doubled, about 45 minutes.

5. With fingertips, make deep indentations (almost to bottom of pan), 1 inch apart, over entire surface of dough. Drizzle dough with remaining 3 tablespoons oil; sprinkle with kosher salt. Cover loosely with plastic wrap; let rise in warm place until doubled, about 45 minutes.

6. Meanwhile, preheat oven to 450°F. Bake focaccia on lowest oven rack until bottom is crusty and top is lightly browned, about 18 minutes. Transfer focaccia to wire rack to cool.

Each serving: About 201 calories, 4g protein, 31g carbohydrate, 7g total fat (1g saturated), 1g fiber, 0mg cholesterol, 537mg sodium.

Red Pepper Focaccia

Prepare Focaccia as directed but do not sprinkle with kosher salt. In 12-inch skillet, heat **1 tablespoon olive oil** over medium heat. Add **4 red peppers**, sliced, and **1/4 teaspoon salt** and cook, stirring frequently, until tender, about 20 minutes. Cool to room temperature. Sprinkle over focaccia just before baking.

Dried Tomato and Olive Focaccia

Prepare Focaccia as directed but do not sprinkle with kosher salt. Combine **1/2 cup Gaeta olives**, pitted, **1/4 cup drained oil-packed dried tomatoes**, coarsely chopped, and **1 1/2 teaspoons kosher salt**. Sprinkle over focaccia just before baking.

Tomato Focaccia

Prepare Focaccia as directed but drizzle with only **1 tablespoon olive oil**. Arrange **1 pound ripe plum tomatoes**, cut into 1/4-inch-thick slices, over top; sprinkle with **1 tablespoon chopped fresh rosemary** or **1 teaspoon dried rosemary**, crumbled, **1/2 teaspoon coarsely ground black pepper**, and **1 teaspoon kosher salt**. Bake as directed.

Onion Focaccia

Prepare Focaccia as directed but do not sprinkle with kosher salt. In 12-inch skillet, heat **2 teaspoons olive oil** over medium heat. Add **2 medium onions**, sliced, **1 teaspoon sugar**, and **1/2 teaspoon salt**, and cook, stirring frequently, until golden brown, about 20 minutes. Cool to room temperature. Spread over focaccia just before baking.

Soft Pretzels

These soft pretzels, a specialty of Pennsylvania Dutch country that has swept the nation, are best served warm with mustard. Freeze them after shaping, if you like. Let them thaw, then dip in the baking-soda mixture and bake as directed. The pretzels can be sprinkled with sesame or poppy seeds in addition to the salt.

PREP: 30 MINUTES PLUS RISING   BAKE: 16 MINUTES   MAKES 12 PRETZELS

2 cups warm water (105° to 115°F)
1 package active dry yeast
1 teaspoon sugar
1 teaspoon salt

about 4 cups all-purpose flour
2 tablespoons baking soda
1 tablespoon kosher or coarse sea salt

1. In large bowl, combine 1 1/2 cups warm water, yeast, and sugar; stir to dissolve. Let stand until foamy, about 5 minutes. Add salt and 2 cups flour; beat well with wooden spoon. Gradually stir in 1 1/2 cups flour to make soft dough.

2. Turn dough onto floured surface and knead until smooth and elastic, about 6 minutes, kneading in enough of remaining 1/2 cup flour just to keep dough from sticking.

3. Shape dough into ball; place in greased large bowl, turning dough to grease top. Cover bowl with plastic wrap and let rise in warm place (80° to 85°F) until doubled in volume, about 30 minutes.

4. Meanwhile, preheat oven to 400°F. Grease two cookie sheets. Punch down dough and cut into 12 equal pieces. Roll each piece into 24-inch-long rope. Shape ropes into loop-shaped pretzels.

5. In small bowl, with wire whisk, whisk remaining 1/2 cup warm water and baking soda until soda dissolves.

6. Dip pretzels in baking-soda mixture and place 1 1/2 inches apart on prepared cookie sheets; sprinkle with kosher salt. Bake until browned, 16 to 18 minutes, rotating cookie sheets between upper and lower oven racks halfway through baking. Serve pretzels warm, or transfer to wire racks to cool.

Each pretzel: About 167 calories, 5g protein, 33g carbohydrate, 1g total fat (0g saturated), 1g fiber, 0mg cholesterol, 1,192mg sodium.

Pissaladière

A specialty of Nice, this flaky pizza-like pie, which is usually served as a snack or appetizer, is a real crowd pleaser. You can prepare the dough a day in advance and refrigerate. Punch dough down; pat into pan and let rise 60 to 90 minutes until almost doubled in bulk.

PREP: 1 HOUR 10 MINUTES PLUS RISING   BAKE: 25 MINUTES
MAKES 32 APPETIZERS

1 cup warm water (105° to 115°F)
1 package active dry yeast
3 cups all-purpose flour
1 3/4 teaspoons salt
2 tablespoons olive oil
2 pounds large yellow onions, cut into 1/2-inch pieces
1 can (2 ounces) anchovy fillets, rinsed, drained, and coarsely chopped
1/3 cup pitted and halved Kalamata or Gaeta olives

1. In cup, combine 1/4 cup warm water and yeast; stir to dissolve. Let stand until foamy, about 5 minutes.

2. In large bowl, combine flour and 1 1/2 teaspoons salt. Stir in yeast mixture, remaining 3/4 cup water, and 1 tablespoon oil. Turn dough onto lightly floured surface and knead until smooth and elastic, about 8 minutes. Shape dough into ball and place in greased large bowl, turning to grease top. Cover with plastic wrap and let rise in warm place (80° to 85°F) until doubled in volume, about 45 minutes.

3. Meanwhile, in 12-inch skillet, heat remaining 1 tablespoon oil over low heat. Add onions and remaining 1/4 teaspoon salt; cook, stirring frequently, until onions are tender, about 30 minutes. Cool to room temperature.

4. Grease 15 1/2" by 10 1/2" jelly-roll pan. Punch down dough and pat into prepared pan. Cover loosely with plastic wrap and let rise 30 minutes.

5. Meanwhile, preheat oven to 425°F. With fingertips, make shallow indentations over surface of dough. Toss onions and anchovies and spread mixture over dough. Place olives on top of onion mixture at 2-inch intervals. Bake on lowest oven rack until crust is golden, about 25 minutes. To serve, cut into 32 squares.

Each appetizer: About 70 calories, 3g protein, 3g carbohydrate, 2g total fat (0g saturated), 1g fiber, 1mg cholesterol, 69mg sodium.

Fired-Up Green-Onion Pancakes

These tempting appetizers are cooked right on the grill for a rustic look and great flavor. If you like, the dough can be prepared through step four up to a day ahead, covered loosely with greased plastic wrap, and refrigerated until you're ready to use it. When you're ready, proceed as directed. Serve with Soy Dipping Sauce on page 49, if you like.

PREP: 20 MINUTES PLUS RISING   GRILL: 4 MINUTES PER BATCH
MAKES 36 APPETIZERS

1 1/4 cups warm water (105° to 115°F)
1 package active dry yeast
1 teaspoon sugar
about 4 1/4 cups all-purpose flour
12 green onions, chopped (about 1 1/3 cups)

1 tablespoon olive oil
1 tablespoon Asian sesame oil
2 teaspoons salt
1 teaspoon coarsely ground black pepper

1. Prepare grill.

2. In large bowl, combine warm water, yeast, and sugar; stir to dissolve. Let stand until foamy, about 5 minutes. Add 1 1/2 cups flour, green onions, olive oil, sesame oil, salt, and pepper. With wooden spoon, stir until blended. Gradually stir in 2 1/2 cups flour to make soft dough. With floured hand, knead mixture in bowl until combined.

3. Turn dough onto lightly floured surface and knead until smooth and elastic, 8 to 10 minutes, working in enough of remaining 1/4 cup flour just to prevent dough from sticking.

4. Shape dough into ball; place in greased large bowl, turning dough to grease top. Cover bowl with greased plastic wrap and let stand in warm place (80° to 85°F) until doubled in volume, about 1 hour.

5. Punch down dough. Turn onto lightly floured surface; cover and let rest 15 minutes.

6. Shape dough into 6 balls. With hand, firmly press each ball into an 8-inch round. Place 3 rounds on grill rack over medium heat; grill until grill marks appear on underside and dough stiffens, 2 to 3 minutes. With tongs, turn rounds and grill until marks appear on underside and pancakes are cooked through, 2 to 3 minutes longer. Repeat with remaining dough.

7. To serve, cut each pancake into 6 wedges.

Each appetizer: About 65 calories, 2g protein, 13g carbohydrate, 1g total fat (0g saturated), 1g fiber, 0mg cholesterol, 120mg sodium.

Romano Toasts

PREP: 5 MINUTES PLUS COOLING   BAKE: 4 MINUTES   MAKES 25 TOASTS

3 ounces shredded Romano or
  Parmesan cheese (1 cup)
1 tablespoon extravirgin olive oil
1 teaspoon fennel seeds, finely
  crushed

1 box (5 ounces) sesame Melba
  toasts (25 toasts)

1. Preheat oven to 400°F. In small bowl, with fork, combine Romano, oil, and fennel seeds. Spread scant tablespoon of cheese mixture on each toast. Transfer toasts to ungreased large cookie sheet.

2. Bake toasts until edges turn golden and cheese melts, 4 to 5 minutes. Cool on cookie sheet on wire rack at least 2 hours to allow topping to dry completely. Store in airtight container up to 1 week.

Each toast: About 40 calories, 2g protein, 4g carbohydrate, 2g total fat (1g saturated), 0g fiber, 3mg cholesterol, 75mg sodium.

Spanakopita

The classic Greek spinach pie with feta cheese and ricotta cheese is accented here with fresh dill.

Prep: 1 hour   Bake: 35 minutes   Makes 24 appetizers

6 tablespoons butter or margarine
1 jumbo onion (1 pound), finely chopped
4 packages (10 ounces each) frozen chopped spinach, thawed and squeezed dry
8 ounces feta cheese, crumbled
1 cup part-skim ricotta cheese

1/2 cup chopped fresh dill
1/4 teaspoon salt
1/4 teaspoon coarsely ground black pepper
3 large eggs
10 sheets (16" by 12" each) fresh or frozen (thawed) phyllo

1. In 12-inch skillet, melt 2 tablespoons butter over medium-high heat until hot. Add onion and cook, stirring occasionally, until tender and lightly browned, about 15 minutes.

2. Transfer onion to large bowl. Stir in spinach, feta, ricotta, dill, salt, pepper, and eggs until combined. Wipe skillet clean.

3. Preheat oven to 400°F. In same skillet, melt remaining 4 tablespoons butter. Remove phyllo from package; keep covered with damp kitchen towel to prevent it from drying out. Lightly brush bottom and sides of 11" by 7" baking dish with some melted butter. On waxed paper, lightly brush 1 phyllo sheet with some melted butter. Place phyllo in baking dish, gently pressing phyllo against sides of dish and allowing it to overhang sides. Lightly brush second sheet with melted butter; place over first sheet. Repeat layering with 3 more phyllo sheets.

4. Spread spinach filling evenly over phyllo in baking dish. Fold overhanging edges of phyllo over filling. Cut remaining 5 phyllo sheets crosswise in half. On waxed paper, lightly brush 1 phyllo sheet with melted butter. Place on top of filling. Repeat with remaining phyllo, brushing each sheet lightly with butter; tuck edges of phyllo under.

5. Bake until filling is hot in center and top of phyllo is golden, 35 to 40 minutes. To serve, cut lengthwise into 4 strips, and then cut each strip crosswise into 6 pieces. Serve hot, warm, or at room temperature.

Each appetizer: 109 calories, 5g protein, 8g carbohydrate, 7g total fat (4g saturated), 2g fiber, 45mg cholesterol, 214mg sodium.

Four-Cheese Pennies

Four fabulous cheeses make this appetizer especially tasty, while a small amount of cornmeal adds just a bit of pleasant crunch.

PREP: 40 MINUTES PLUS COOLING BAKE: 18 MINUTES PER BATCH
MAKES ABOUT 90 PENNIES

2 tablespoons sesame seeds or
  1/4 cup pecans, finely chopped
1 1/2 cups all-purpose flour
1/2 cup yellow cornmeal
1 teaspoon dry mustard
3/4 teaspoon salt
1/4 teaspoon ground red pepper
  (cayenne)
3/4 cup butter (1 1/2 sticks), softened
  (do not use margarine)

4 ounces extrasharp Cheddar cheese,
  shredded (1 cup)
2 ounces Gouda cheese, shredded
  (1/2 cup)
1 ounce Fontina cheese, shredded
  (1/4 cup)
1/4 cup freshly grated Parmesan
  cheese

1. Preheat oven to 375°F. Line large cookie sheet with parchment paper.
2. In small skillet, heat sesame seeds over medium heat, shaking skillet frequently, until toasted, 2 to 3 minutes. Transfer sesame seeds to cup; cool.
3. In medium bowl, combine flour, cornmeal, mustard, salt, and ground red pepper. In large bowl, with mixer at medium speed, beat butter, Cheddar, Gouda, Fontina, and Parmesan until blended. Reduce mixer speed to low; add flour mixture and beat until dough is evenly moistened and begins to hold together.
4. Shape dough by measuring teaspoons into 3/4-inch balls. Place balls 1 inch apart on prepared cookie sheet. With tines of fork, press each ball to flatten slightly; sprinkle with sesame seeds.
5. Bake pennies until golden, 18 to 20 minutes. Transfer to wire rack to cool completely. Store in airtight container at room temperature up to 5 days or in freezer up to 3 months.

Each penny: About 35 calories, 1g protein, 2g carbohydrate, 3g total fat (2g saturated), 0g fiber, 7mg cholesterol, 55mg sodium.

Caraway-Cheese Crisps

Store these treats in an airtight container up to three days.

PREP: 20 MINUTES BAKE: 10 MINUTES PER BATCH
MAKES ABOUT 54 CRISPS

**12 ounces extrasharp Cheddar
cheese, shredded (3 cups)**
1 1/2 cups all-purpose flour
**1/2 cup butter or margarine (1 stick),
softened**

1/2 teaspoon caraway seeds
1/4 teaspoon salt

1. Preheat oven to 425°F. In large bowl, with hand, knead Cheddar, flour, butter, caraway seeds, and salt until blended.
2. Divide dough into 3 equal pieces. Shape 1 dough piece into 1/2-inch balls. Place balls 2 inches apart on ungreased cookie sheet. With fingers, flatten balls to 1/4-inch thickness.
3. Bake until lightly browned, 10 to 12 minutes. With spatula, transfer cheese crisps to wire racks to cool. Repeat with remaining dough.

Each crisp: About 53 calories, 2g protein, 3g carbohydrate, 4g total fat (2g saturated), 0g fiber, 11mg cholesterol, 67mg sodium.

Swiss Cheese Crisps

Prepare as directed but substitute **Swiss cheese** for Cheddar cheese and add **1/8 teaspoon ground red pepper (cayenne)** to cheese mixture.

Pecorino and Pepper Coins

Bet you can't eat just one of these palette teasers! You can freeze unbaked logs for up to three months. Slice and bake when needed.

PREP: 50 MINUTES PLUS COOLING BAKE: 15 MINUTES PER BATCH
MAKES ABOUT 312 COINS

1/2 cup dry white wine
2 1/4 cups all-purpose flour
1 1/2 cups finely grated Pecorino-
  Romano cheese
2 teaspoons kosher salt

1 cup butter or margarine (2 sticks),
  softened
2 tablespoons sugar
1 tablespoon coarsely ground pepper

1. In 1-cup microwave-safe cup or bowl, heat wine in microwave on High 6 to 7 minutes, or until reduced to 1 tablespoon. Cool 10 minutes in refrigerator.

2. On waxed paper, combine flour, 1 cup Pecorino, and salt. In large bowl, with mixer at medium speed, beat butter and sugar until creamy, about 2 minutes; beat in wine until blended. With mixer at low speed, beat in flour mixture until blended.

3. On 16-inch length of waxed paper, combine pepper with remaining 1/2 cup Pecorino.

4. Divide dough into 12 equal pieces (each about heaping 1/4 cup). Roll each piece into 13" by 1/2" log. Roll logs in cheese mixture. Wrap each log in plastic wrap and slide onto cookie sheet for easier handling. Freeze until dough is firm enough to slice, at least 15 minutes. (Or, place dough in refrigerator about 1 hour.)

5. Meanwhile, preheat oven to 350°F. Line 2 cookie sheets with parchment paper.

6. Remove 1 log from freezer; discard plastic wrap. Cut log into 1/2-inch-thick coins. Place coins 1/2 inch apart on prepared cookie sheet. Repeat with 5 logs to fill one cookie sheet.

7. Bake coins until golden, 15 to 20 minutes. Slide parchment onto wire rack; cool coins completely. Repeat with remaining logs. Store coins at room temperature in airtight container up to 1 week or in freezer up to 3 months.

Each 1/4 cup coins: About 205 calories, 4g protein, 16g carbohydrate, 14g total fat (3g saturated), 1g fiber, 8mg cholesterol, 480mg sodium.

Samosas

These curried vegetable turnovers are usually deep-fried, but we like these flavorful treats best when baked.

PREP: 1 HOUR 20 MINUTES BAKE: 12 MINUTES PER BATCH
MAKES ABOUT 54 TURNOVERS

FLAKY PASTRY
3 cups all-purpose flour
1¹⁄₂ teaspoons baking powder
³⁄₄ teaspoon salt
1 cup vegetable shortening
about 6 tablespoons ice water

VEGETABLE FILLING
1 tablespoon vegetable oil
1 medium onion, finely chopped
2 medium all-purpose potatoes,
  chopped (1¹⁄₂ cups)
1 tablespoon minced, peeled fresh
  ginger

1 large garlic clove, finely chopped
1 teaspoon curry powder
¹⁄₂ teaspoon ground cumin
¹⁄₄ teaspoon ground red pepper
  (cayenne)
1 cup water
1 teaspoon salt
¹⁄₂ cup frozen baby peas
¹⁄₄ cup chopped fresh cilantro
1 large egg beaten with 2
  tablespoons water

1. Prepare flaky pastry: In large bowl, combine flour, baking powder, and salt. With pastry blender or two knives used scissor-fashion, cut in shortening until mixture resembles coarse crumbs. Sprinkle with water, 1 tablespoon at a time, mixing lightly with fork after each addition, until dough is just moist enough to hold together. Shape dough into ball. Wrap in waxed paper and refrigerate while preparing filling or up to overnight.

2. In 10-inch skillet, heat oil over medium heat. Add onion and cook, stirring frequently, until tender, about 5 minutes. Add potatoes and cook, stirring frequently, until onion begins to brown, about 10 minutes.

3. Stir in ginger, garlic, curry powder, cumin, and ground red pepper and cook 30 seconds. Add water and salt; heat to boiling. Reduce heat; cover and simmer until potatoes are tender, 10 to 15 minutes. Stir in frozen peas and cook, uncovered, until liquid has evaporated. Remove from heat and add cilantro, mashing potatoes coarsely with back of spoon.

4. Preheat oven to 425°F. Divide dough into 4 equal pieces. On floured surface, with floured rolling pin, roll 1 piece of dough 1/16 inch thick. Keep remaining dough covered. With 3-inch biscuit cutter, cut out as many rounds as possible, reserving trimmings. On one half of each dough round, place 1 level teaspoon filling. Brush edges of rounds with some beaten egg mixture. Fold dough over to enclose filling. With fork, press edges together to seal dough; prick top. Brush turnovers lightly with some beaten egg mixture. With spatula, lift turnovers and arrange 1 inch apart on ungreased large cookie sheet.

5. Bake turnovers until just golden, 12 to 15 minutes. Repeat with remaining dough, filling, and beaten egg mixture. Serve hot or warm.

Each turnover: About 62 calories, 1g protein, 6g carbohydrate, 4g total fat (1g saturated), 0g fiber, 4mg cholesterol, 84mg sodium.

Savory Blue Cheese, Walnut, and Date Rugelach

A rich cream-cheese dough is the perfect match for the delicious savory filling of walnuts, blue cheese, and dates. Plan to make them for your next party; they can be frozen for up to three months. Arrange the unbaked rugelach in a single layer in a jelly-roll pan, then cover and freeze until firm. Transfer the rugelach to freezer containers with waxed paper between each layer; seal, label, and freeze. About forty-five minutes before serving, preheat oven to 350°F. Place the frozen rugelach on greased cookie sheets and bake until golden, about thirty-five minutes.

PREP: 40 MINUTES PLUS CHILLING AND COOLING   BAKE: 30 MINUTES
MAKES 48 APPETIZERS

1 cup butter or margarine (2 sticks), softened
1 package (8 ounces) cream cheese, softened
2 cups all-purpose flour
1/2 teaspoon salt

1 1/2 cups walnuts (6 ounces)
4 ounces blue cheese, cut into chunks
48 pitted dates (about 12 ounces)
1 large egg white beaten with 1 teaspoon water

1. Prepare rugelach dough: In large bowl, with mixer at medium speed, beat butter and cream cheese until creamy, occasionally scraping bowl with rubber spatula. Reduce speed to low; gradually beat in flour and salt just until blended, occasionally scraping bowl.

2. Divide dough into 4 equal pieces; flatten each into a disk. Wrap each disk in plastic wrap and refrigerate until dough is firm enough to roll, at least 4 hours or up to overnight. (Or place dough in freezer 1 hour if using butter, 1 1/2 hours if using margarine.)

3. In food processor with knife blade attached, pulse 1/2 cup walnuts until finely chopped; transfer to small bowl. In food processor (no need to clean it), pulse blue cheese and remaining 1 cup walnuts 7 to 8 times, or until a coarse mixture forms.

4. Preheat oven to 350°F. Line 2 large cookie sheets with foil; grease foil.

5. On lightly floured surface, with floured rolling pin, roll 1 disk of dough into 10-inch round. (If dough is too cold to roll, let stand 5 to 10 minutes at room temperature to soften slightly.) With pastry wheel or knife, cut round into 12 wedges. Beginning 1 inch from edge of dough round, sprinkle 1/2 cup blue-cheese mixture in 2-inch-wide ring over dough, leaving dough in center exposed. Place 1 date crosswise on wide end of each wedge. Starting at wide end, roll up each wedge, jelly-roll fashion.

6. Place rugelach 1 inch apart on prepared cookie sheets, point side down. Repeat with remaining dough, blue-cheese mixture, and dates. Brush rugelach with egg white mixture; sprinkle with reserved walnuts.

7. Bake rugelach until golden, 30 to 35 minutes, rotating sheets between upper and lower oven racks halfway through baking. Transfer to wire racks to cool. Store rugelach in airtight container at room temperature up to 3 days, or in freezer up to 3 months.

Each appetizer: About 125 calories, 2g protein, 10g carbohydrate, 9g total fat (4g saturated), 1g fiber, 18mg cholesterol, 115mg sodium.

Mushroom Turnovers

These tender pastries are made with an easy cream-cheese dough.

PREP: 1 HOUR PLUS COOLING AND FREEZING   COOK/BAKE: 32 MINUTES
MAKES ABOUT 48 TURNOVERS

FLAKY CREAM-CHEESE PASTRY
1 1/2 cups all-purpose flour
1 package (8 ounces) cream cheese, softened
1/2 cup butter or margarine (1 stick), softened

MUSHROOM FILLING
3 tablespoons butter or margarine
1 medium onion, finely chopped
8 ounces white mushrooms, trimmed and chopped

1 garlic clove, crushed with garlic press
1 tablespoon all-purpose flour
1/2 teaspoon salt
1/4 teaspoon coarsely ground black pepper
1/4 teaspoon dried thyme
1 tablespoon dry sherry or dry vermouth
3 tablespoons sour cream
1 large egg beaten with 2 tablespoons water

1. Prepare flaky cream-cheese pastry: In medium bowl, with hand, knead flour, cream cheese, and butter until blended. Shape dough into 2 disks; wrap each with plastic wrap and refrigerate until firm enough to handle, about 30 minutes.

2. Meanwhile, prepare mushroom filling: In 12-inch skillet, melt butter over medium heat. Add onion and mushrooms and cook, stirring frequently, until onion is tender and liquid has evaporated, about 20 minutes. Stir in garlic, flour, salt, pepper, and thyme; add sherry and cook 1 minute longer. Transfer mixture to bowl; cool. Stir in sour cream.

3. On floured surface, with floured rolling pin, roll 1 disk of dough 1/8 inch thick. With 3-inch biscuit cutter, cut out as many rounds as possible, reserving trimmings.

4. On one half of each dough round, place 1 rounded measuring teaspoon filling. Brush edges of rounds with some beaten egg mixture. Fold dough over to enclose filling. With fork, press edges together to seal dough. Brush turnovers lightly with egg mixture; prick tops. Place turnovers about 1 inch apart on ungreased cookie sheet.

5. Repeat with remaining dough, trimmings, and filling to make about 48 turnovers in all.

6. Cover cookie sheets tightly with plastic wrap or foil and refrigerate turnovers up to 1 day. Or, to freeze, place unbaked turnovers in jelly-roll pan; cover and freeze until firm. With wide spatula, transfer turnovers to freezer-safe containers with waxed paper between each layer; freeze up to 1 month.

7. Preheat oven to 450°F. Bake cold turnovers until golden and heated through, 12 to 14 minutes. Or, place frozen turnovers 1 inch apart on ungreased cookie sheets and bake until golden, 15 to 20 minutes. Serve hot or warm.

Each turnover: About 60 calories, 1g protein, 4g carbohydrate, 5g total fat (3g saturated), 0g fiber, 17mg cholesterol, 545mg sodium.

Mushroom Turnovers

Mushroom-Filled Toast Cups

You can prepare the toast cups several hours or up to a day ahead. Be sure that the bread you use is very fresh (look at the expiration date) or it will crack.

PREP: 45 MINUTES BAKE: 16 MINUTES
MAKES 24 MUSHROOM TOAST CUPS

24 slices very thin white bread, crusts trimmed

2 tablespoons butter or margarine, melted

1 tablespoon olive oil

1 small onion, finely chopped

2 garlic cloves, finely chopped

1 small red pepper, finely chopped

6 ounces shiitake mushrooms, stems removed and caps coarsely chopped

6 ounces white mushrooms, trimmed and coarsely chopped

1/4 teaspoon salt

1/4 teaspoon ground black pepper

1 tablespoon all-purpose flour

3/4 cup half-and-half or light cream

1. Preheat oven to 375°F. Lightly grease twenty-four 1³/₄-inch by 1-inch mini muffin-pan cups. Gently fit the bread into prepared muffin-pan cups. Lightly brush with butter. Bake until golden, 8 to 10 minutes.

2. In 12-inch skillet, heat oil over medium heat. Add onion and garlic and cook, stirring frequently, until tender, about 5 minutes. Add red pepper and cook until tender, about 4 minutes longer.

3. Add shiitake and white mushrooms, salt, and pepper; cook, stirring frequently, until mushrooms are tender, about 5 minutes. Stir in flour until coated. Gradually add half-and-half; heat to boiling. Boil until mixture has thickened slightly, about 2 minutes. Spoon into prepared toast cups. Bake until heated through, about 8 minutes.

Each mushroom toast cup: About 102 calories, 3g protein, 16g carbohydrate, 3g total fat (1g saturated), 0g fiber, 5mg cholesterol, 165mg sodium.

Spinach-Feta Cups

Preheat oven to 375°F. Prepare toast cups as directed. In 8-inch skillet heat **1 teaspoon olive oil** over medium heat. Add **2 green onions, thinly sliced**, and cook, stirring frequently, until tender, about 1 minute. Transfer to medium bowl; stir in **1 package (10 ounces) frozen chopped spinach, thawed and squeezed dry**, **1/2 teaspoon dried mint, crumbled,** and 1/4 **teaspoon salt**. Spoon into 24 prepared toast cups and sprinkle with **2 ounces feta cheese, crumbled (¹/2 cup).** Bake until heated through, 8 to 10 minutes. Makes 24 toast cups.

Each spinach toast cup: About 90 calories, 3g protein, 15g carbohydrate, 3g total fat (1g saturated), 0g fiber, 5mg cholesterol, 216mg sodium.

Mini Crab Cakes

Mini Crab Cakes

Crab cakes are a universal favorite. These luscious morsels can be prepared ahead and refrigerated. Bake just before serving.

PREP: 25 MINUTES   BAKE: 16 MINUTES   MAKES 40 MINI CRAB CAKES

Lemon Sauce (below)
1/4 cup mayonnaise
1 tablespoon sour cream
2 teaspoons grainy Dijon mustard
1/2 teaspoon freshly grated lemon
  peel

1/4 teaspoon salt
1/8 teaspoon ground red pepper
  (cayenne)
1 pound lump crabmeat, picked over
1 cup fresh bread crumbs (about 2
  slices bread)

1. Preheat oven to 400°F. Lightly grease large cookie sheet. Prepare Lemon Sauce; cover and refrigerate.

2. In medium bowl, stir mayonnaise, sour cream, mustard, lemon peel, salt, and ground red pepper until blended; stir in crabmeat and bread crumbs just until mixed.

3. Drop level tablespoons crab mixture on prepared cookie sheet. Bake until golden brown, 16 to 18 minutes. Top each crab cake with about 1/2 teaspoon lemon sauce. Serve hot.

Each crab cake with sauce: About 30 calories, 2g protein, 1g carbohydrate, 2g total fat (0g saturated), 0g fiber, 13mg cholesterol, 70mg sodium.

Lemon Sauce

In small bowl, stir **1/2 cup sour cream**, **1 teaspoon freshly grated lemon peel**, **pinch salt**, and **pinch ground red pepper (cayenne)** until blended. Makes about 1/2 cup.

Scalloped Oysters

This flavorful first course consists of juicy oysters tossed with buttery crumbs and heavy cream and is baked in individual ramekins. You can toast the bread up to two days ahead and keep tightly sealed in a plastic bag.

PREP: 15 MINUTES BAKE: 40 MINUTES
MAKES 8 FIRST-COURSE SERVINGS

10 slices firm white bread, torn into 1-inch pieces
4 tablespoons butter or margarine, melted
1 1/2 pints shucked oysters
3/4 cup heavy or whipping cream
1/4 teaspoon salt
1/8 teaspoon coarsely ground black pepper
2 tablespoons chopped fresh parsley

1. Preheat oven to 400°F. Spread bread pieces into 15 1/2" by 10 1/2" jelly-roll pan; drizzle with melted butter and toss to coat. Bake, stirring occasionally, until golden and crisp, about 25 minutes.

2. Meanwhile, drain oysters, reserving oyster liquor. In 1-quart saucepan, heat oyster liquor to boiling over high heat. Reduce heat to medium and cook liquor until reduced to about 3 tablespoons, about 5 minutes. Add cream, salt, and pepper; heat to boiling. Remove from heat.

3. In large bowl, toss together toasted bread pieces, oysters, and parsley. Spoon mixture into eight 12-ounce ramekins; pour about 2 tablespoons cream mixture over each. Bake until oysters turn opaque throughout, 15 minutes.

Each serving: About 260 calories, 8g protein, 20g carbohydrate, 17g total fat (7g saturated), 0g fiber, 55mg cholesterol, 465mg sodium.

Ham Biscuits

If you like, prepare and refrigerate the flour-shortening mixture early in the day, then add the milk right before mixing. When cutting out the biscuits, press the cutter straight down: Do not twist it, or the biscuits might turn out lopsided.

PREP: 15 MINUTES   BAKE: 12 MINUTES
MAKES ABOUT 18 HIGH BISCUITS OR 36 THIN BISCUITS

2 cups all-purpose flour
1 tablespoon baking powder
1/2 teaspoon salt
1/4 cup vegetable shortening

3/4 cup milk
softened butter
9 ounces thinly sliced country-style ham

1. Preheat oven to 450°F. In large bowl, combine flour, baking powder, and salt. With pastry blender or two knives used scissor-fashion, cut in vegetable shortening until mixture resembles coarse crumbs. Stir in milk, stirring just until mixture forms soft dough that leaves side of bowl.

2. Turn dough onto lightly floured surface; knead just until smooth, 6 to 8 times. With floured rolling pin, roll dough 1/2 inch thick for high, fluffy biscuits or 1/4 inch thick for thin, crusty biscuits.

3. With floured 2-inch biscuit cutter, cut out rounds, without twisting cutter. Arrange biscuits on ungreased cookie sheet, 1 inch apart for crusty biscuits or nearly touching for soft-sided biscuits.

4. Press trimmings together; reroll and cut out additional biscuits. Bake until golden, 12 to 15 minutes. Allow to cool.

5. Split biscuits in half. Spread each half with butter and top with ham.

Each high biscuit: About 123 calories, 4g protein, 12g carbohydrate, 7g total fat (4g saturated), 0g fiber, 22mg cholesterol, 275mg sodium.

FINGER FOODS

Panfried Steak and Onions on Grilled Bread

Roasted Peppers with Fresh Basil

Try these colorful peppers with any of our suggested toppings or mix a few together.

PREP: 35 MINUTES   ROAST: 8 MINUTES   MAKES 6 APPETIZER SERVINGS

2 large red peppers
2 large yellow peppers
1 tablespoon extravirgin olive oil
1/4 teaspoon salt

1/8 teaspoon ground black pepper
3 large fresh basil leaves, thinly
  sliced

1. Roast peppers: Preheat broiler. Line broiling pan with foil. Cut each red and yellow pepper lengthwise in half; remove and discard stems and seeds. Arrange peppers, cut side down, in prepared pan. Place pan in broiler, 5 to 6 inches from heat source. Broil peppers, without turning, until skin is charred and blistered, 8 to 10 minutes.

2. Wrap peppers in foil and allow to steam at room temperature 15 minutes or until cool enough to handle.

3. Remove peppers from foil. Peel skin and discard. Cut peppers lengthwise into 1/2-inch-wide strips. Pat dry with paper towels.

4. Place pepper strips on platter; drizzle with oil and sprinkle with salt and black pepper. To serve, sprinkle with basil leaves, or cover and refrigerate up to overnight.

Each serving without additional toppings: About 38 calories, 1g protein, 4g carbohydrate, 2g total fat (0g saturated), 2g fiber, 0mg cholesterol, 97mg sodium.

Additional Toppings

- Chopped fresh parsley, oregano, mint, chives, sage, marjoram, rosemary, or savory, or a combination
- Drained capers
- Finely chopped red onion
- Drained and chopped anchovy fillets
- Minced garlic
- Crushed red pepper
- Chopped pitted Kalamata or Gaeta olives
- Crumbled feta cheese

Stuffed Pepperoncini

Tuscan peppers, available in jars on the grocer's shelf, are slightly hot and just the right size to pop into your mouth. In this tasty recipe, the heat from the peppers is complemented by the smokiness of the bacon and the silky mildness of the cream cheese.

PREP: 25 MINUTES   COOK: 11 MINUTES   MAKES ABOUT 28 APPETIZERS

3 slices bacon, finely chopped
2 large shallots, minced ($1/4$ cup)
$1/2$ medium red pepper, minced ($1/3$ cup)
1 package (3 ounces) cream cheese, softened

2 teaspoons milk
2 jars ($9 1/2$ to 10 ounces each) Tuscan or pepperoncini peppers, drained (28 peppers)

1. In nonstick 10-inch skillet, cook bacon over medium-low heat until browned, about 7 minutes. With slotted spoon, transfer bacon to paper towels to drain. Discard all but 1 tablespoon bacon drippings from skillet.

2. In drippings in skillet, cook shallots and red pepper over medium heat, stirring frequently, until tender, about 4 minutes. Remove from heat.

3. In small bowl, with mixer at medium speed, beat cream cheese and milk until smooth. Add bacon and shallot mixture and beat just until combined. Spoon into zip-tight plastic bag with a corner cut to make $1/4$-inch opening. With small knife, cut long lengthwise slit in each pepper. Pipe cream-cheese mixture into peppers. Arrange on platter; cover and refrigerate up to 1 day.

Each appetizer: About 20 calories, 1g protein, 1g carbohydrate, 1g total fat (1g saturated), 0g fiber, 4mg cholesterol, 338mg sodium.

Roman-Style Artichokes

PREP: 25 MINUTES   COOK: 40 MINUTES
MAKES 8 FIRST-COURSE SERVINGS

8 medium artichokes
1 lemon, cut in half
1/4 cup extravirgin olive oil
6 large mint sprigs plus 1/2 cup
   loosely packed fresh mint leaves,
   chopped

3 large garlic cloves, finely chopped
2 cups water
1/2 cup dry white wine
1/2 teaspoon salt
1/4 teaspoon ground black pepper

1. Trim artichokes: Bend back outer green leaves from around base of artichoke and snap off. With kitchen shears, trim thorny tops from remaining outer leaves, rubbing all cut surfaces with lemon half to prevent browning. Lay artichoke on its side and cut off stem, level with bottom of artichoke. Peel stem; place in bowl of *cold water* and juice of remaining lemon half. Cut 1 inch off top of artichoke; add artichoke to lemon water. Repeat with remaining artichokes.

2. In nonreactive 8-quart Dutch oven or saucepot, heat oil over medium heat until hot. Add mint sprigs and garlic and cook, stirring frequently, until garlic is golden, about 3 minutes. Add water, wine, salt, and pepper; heat to boiling over high heat.

3. Reduce heat to medium. Stand artichokes in boiling liquid; add stems. Cover and simmer until knife inserted in bottom of artichoke goes in easily, 30 to 40 minutes.

4. Place artichokes and stems in 8 shallow soup bowls. Discard mint sprigs; spoon cooking liquid over artichokes. Sprinkle with chopped mint.

5. To eat, starting at bottom of artichoke, pluck off leaves one by one. Dip leaves in broth and pull through your teeth, scraping off pulp. Place leaves in separate dish or plate. When leaves are too small and thin to eat, pull them out to reveal fuzzy choke. With tip of spoon, scrape out choke and discard. Cut solid heart into chunks to eat.

Each serving: About 125 calories, 4g protein, 14g carbohydrate, 7g total fat (1g saturated), 7g fiber, 0mg cholesterol, 260mg sodium.

Roman-Style Artichokes

Pickled Vegetables

Each vegetable is marinated with different herbs and spices; together they create an extra-special relish tray.

PREP: 30 MINUTES PLUS OVERNIGHT TO CHILL   COOK: 20 MINUTES
MAKES 12 APPETIZER SERVINGS

2 bags (16 ounces each) carrots, peeled and cut into 4" by 1/4" matchstick strips
1 pound green beans, trimmed
1 medium head cauliflower (2 pounds), separated into flowerets
1 small bunch celery, cut into 4" by 1/2" matchstick strips
3 cups cider vinegar
1 cup water
1/4 cup chopped fresh dill or 2 teaspoons dried dill weed

1/3 cup sugar
2 teaspoons salt
1 teaspoon whole black peppercorns
peel of 1 small orange removed in strips
1 teaspoon fennel seeds, crushed
1 tablespoon pickling spice
peel of 1 lemon removed in strips
1 teaspoon dried tarragon
8 ounces green or black olives
2 bunches radishes, trimmed

1. In 4-quart saucepan, heat *2 inches water* to boiling over high heat. Add carrots; heat to boiling. Cook until tender-crisp, 1 to 2 minutes. With slotted spoon, transfer carrots to bowl of cold water to stop cooking; drain well. Repeat with green beans and cauliflower. Place each vegetable in a separate zip-tight plastic bag. Place unblanched celery in zip-tight plastic bag.

2. Prepare peppercorn-dill carrot marinade: In 1-cup measuring cup, combine 3/4 cup vinegar, 1/4 cup water, dill, 4 teaspoons sugar, 1/2 teaspoon salt, and peppercorns. Add to carrots; close bag.

3. Prepare orange-fennel green bean marinade: In 1-cup measuring cup, combine 3/4 cup vinegar, 1/4 cup water, orange strips, 4 teaspoons sugar, fennel seeds, and 1/2 teaspoon salt. Add to green beans; close bag.

4. Prepare spiced cauliflower marinade: In 1-cup measuring cup, combine 3/4 cup vinegar, 1/4 cup water, 4 teaspoons sugar, pickling spice, and 1/2 teaspoon salt. Add to cauliflower; close bag.

5. Prepare lemon-tarragon celery marinade. In 1-cup measuring cup, combine ³/4 cup vinegar, ¹/4 cup water, lemon strips, 4 teaspoons sugar, tarragon, and ¹/2 teaspoon salt. Add to celery; close bag.

6. Refrigerate bags at least 8 hours or up to 2 days, turning bags occasionally.

7. To serve, drain marinade from each vegetable. Arrange pickled vegetables on large tray or platter with olives and radishes.

Each serving: About 90 calories, 3g protein, 16g carbohydrate, 4g total fat (0g saturated), 5g fiber, 0mg cholesterol, 240mg sodium.

Prosciutto with Melon

The marriage of sweet, ripe melon and slightly salty prosciutto is a classic combination. Imported prosciutto di Parma, available at Italian grocers and specialty food markets, is much milder than domestic varieties of this ham. It's worth seeking out.

PREP: 10 MINUTES   MAKES 4 FIRST-COURSE SERVINGS

1 small honeydew melon or 1 medium cantaloupe, chilled	**4 ounces thinly sliced prosciutto ground black pepper**

1. Cut melon in half through stem end; remove and discard seeds. Cut each half into 4 wedges; cut off rind.

2. Arrange 2 melon wedges on each plate. Place prosciutto to one side of melon. Sprinkle with pepper.

Each serving: About 150 calories, 9g protein, 22g carbohydrate, 4g total fat (1g saturated), 2g fiber, 23mg cholesterol, 548mg sodium.

Prosciutto with Other Fruit

Prepare as directed but substitute **8 large green or black figs**, each cut in half, or **2 medium papayas, nectarines, mangoes, pears, or apples,** peeled, seeded, and sliced, for melon.

Roasted Prosciutto-Wrapped Asparagus

Roasted Prosciutto–Wrapped Asparagus

You can oven-steam the asparagus in advance, wrap with the ham and cheese, and refrigerate up to 8 hours. Roast the wrapped spears just before serving.

PREP: 30 MINUTES STEAM/ROAST: 20 MINUTES MAKES 24 APPETIZERS

24 medium asparagus spears (about 1 1/2 pounds), trimmed
12 thin slices prosciutto (8 ounces), each cut lengthwise in half
1/2 cup freshly grated Parmesan cheese

1. Preheat oven to 400°F. Place asparagus and *1/4 cup boiling water* in large roasting pan (17" by 11 1/2"); cover pan with foil. Place in oven and steam asparagus until tip of knife goes easily into thicker end of stem, 10 to 15 minutes. With tongs, transfer asparagus to paper towels to drain. Wipe pan dry.

2. On waxed paper, place 1 strip prosciutto; sprinkle with 1 teaspoon Parmesan. Place asparagus spear on 1 end of prosciutto strip. Roll prosciutto around asparagus spear, slightly overlapping prosciutto as you roll, and covering most of spear. Repeat with remaining asparagus, prosciutto, and Parmesan.

3. Place wrapped asparagus in roasting pan (it's all right if spears touch), and roast until asparagus is heated through and prosciutto just begins to brown, about 10 minutes.

Each appetizer: About 25 calories, 4g protein, 1g carbohydrate, 1g total fat (1g saturated), 0g fiber, 8mg cholesterol, 270mg sodium.

Black Forest Ham–Wrapped Asparagus

Prepare as directed but substitute **12 thin slices Black Forest ham (about 8 ounces)** for prosciutto and use **1 cup shredded Gruyère cheese** (about 1 1/2 teaspoons per spear) for Parmesan.

Each appetizer: About 40 calories, 4g protein, 1g carbohydrate, 3g total fat (1g saturated), 0g fiber, 11mg cholesterol, 158mg sodium.

Chesapeake Bay Crab-Stuffed Mushrooms

Mushrooms can be stuffed early in the day and refrigerated until ready to bake. Increase baking time to 15 minutes covered, 10 minutes uncovered.

PREP: 45 MINUTES BAKE: 20 MINUTES MAKES 8 FIRST-COURSE SERVINGS

24 large white mushrooms (2-inch diameter) with stems, trimmed
3 tablespoons butter or margarine
1 small onion, finely chopped
1 large stalk celery, finely chopped
1 tablespoon all-purpose flour
1/2 teaspoon salt

1/4 teaspoon coarsely ground black pepper
1 cup milk
2 tablespoons dry sherry
2 slices white bread, coarsely grated
8 ounces lump crabmeat, picked over
2 tablespoons chopped fresh parsley

1. Remove stems from mushrooms; chop stems. If necessary, cut a very thin slice from rounded side of each cap so they stand flat. Place mushroom caps, stem side up, in 15 1/2" by 10 1/2" jelly-roll pan.

2. Preheat oven to 400°F. In 10-inch skillet, melt butter over medium heat. Add onion, celery, and mushroom stems; cook, stirring occasionally until vegetables are tender and golden, 15 to 20 minutes.

3. Increase heat to medium-high. Sprinkle flour, salt, and pepper over vegetable mixture. Cook, stirring constantly, 1 minute. Gradually stir in milk, then sherry; heat to boiling, stirring constantly. Remove from heat. Add bread crumbs, crabmeat, and 1 tablespoon parsley, stirring to mix well and break up crabmeat slightly.

4. Fill mushrooms with crabmeat mixture. Spray large sheet of foil with nonstick cooking spray. Place foil, greased side down, on top of mushrooms. Bake mushrooms 10 minutes. Remove foil and bake 10 minutes longer. Sprinkle with remaining 1 tablespoon parsley. Serve hot.

Each serving: About 125 calories, 9g protein, 10g carbohydrate, 6g total fat (1g saturated), 1g fiber, 19mg cholesterol, 550mg sodium.

Savory Stuffed Mushrooms

PREP: 45 MINUTES   BAKE: 15 MINUTES   MAKES 12 APPETIZER SERVINGS

1 cup fresh bread crumbs (about 2
   slices bread)
1 1/2 pounds medium cremini or white
   mushrooms (about 3 1/2 dozen),
   trimmed
4 slices bacon
1/2 small red pepper, finely chopped
1 small stalk celery, finely chopped
2 large shallots, finely chopped
   (about 1/4 cup)

1/2 teaspoon finely chopped fresh
   thyme
1/4 teaspoon coarsely ground black
   pepper
2 ounces mild goat cheese, such as
   Montrachet, crumbled (1/3 cup)
2 tablespoons chopped fresh parsley

1. Preheat oven to 375°F. Spread bread crumbs in 15 1/2" by 10 1/2" jelly-roll pan; bake until golden, 5 to 6 minutes. Transfer to large bowl; cool. Wipe pan clean.

2. Meanwhile, remove stems from mushrooms; finely chop stems. Spray same jelly-roll pan with nonstick cooking spray. Arrange mushroom caps, stem side down, in pan. Bake until mushrooms release their liquid, about 10 minutes. Transfer mushrooms, stem side down, to paper towels to drain.

3. In 12-inch skillet, cook bacon over medium heat until browned. Transfer to paper towels to drain.

4. Discard all but 1 tablespoon bacon fat from skillet; increase heat to medium-high. Add mushroom stems and cook until golden, about 3 minutes. Add red pepper, celery, shallots, thyme, and black pepper; cook until vegetables are tender, about 5 minutes. Remove from heat and cool slightly.

5. Coarsely crumble bacon. Add bacon, vegetables, goat cheese, and parsley to bread crumbs in bowl; stir until well combined.

6. Wash and dry same jelly-roll pan; spray with nonstick cooking spray. Place mushroom caps, stem side up, in pan; spoon stuffing mixture into caps. Bake until stuffing is golden brown, 15 to 20 minutes. Serve hot or warm.

Each serving: About 70 calories, 5g protein, 5g carbohydrate, 3g total fat (2g saturated), 2g fiber, 5mg cholesterol, 100mg sodium.

Cheddar and Green-Onion Potato Skins

These fun appetizers are just like those found on restaurant menus, but these are even better! If you like, cook the unused portion of potato and turn it into mashed potatoes. For a change, try our pizza or Brie-and-chutney variations.

PREP: 15 MINUTES BAKE: 35 MINUTES MAKES 16 POTATO SKINS

4 medium baking potatoes (8 ounces each)
1 tablespoon olive oil
1 teaspoon salt
$1/2$ teaspoon coarsely ground black pepper

$3/4$ cup shredded sharp Cheddar cheese
2 green onions, thinly sliced
sour cream (optional)

1. Preheat oven to 475°F. Cut each potato lengthwise into quarters. With small knife, cut away some potato flesh from each quarter, leaving $3/4$-inch-thick shell. (Reserve potato flesh for another use.)
2. Place potato skins in $15\,1/2"$ by $10\,1/2"$ jelly-roll pan; toss with oil to coat. Arrange potato skins, skin side down, in single layer in pan; sprinkle with salt and pepper. Bake until potato skins are fork-tender and golden, about 30 minutes. Remove pan from oven. Sprinkle Cheddar, then green onions over potato skins. Bake until cheese melts, about 5 minutes longer. Top each with a dollop of sour cream, if you like.

Each potato skin: About 70 calories, 2g protein, 10g carbohydrate, 3g total fat (1g saturated), 2g fiber, 6mg cholesterol, 185mg sodium.

Pizza Skins

Prepare potato skins as directed through step 2. Top skins with **1 cup jarred spaghetti sauce**, then **3 ounces mozzarella cheese, shredded ($3/4$ cup)**. Bake until cheese melts, about 5 minutes.

Each potato skin: About 80 calories, 3g protein, 13g carbohydrate, 3g total fat (1g saturated), 2g fiber, 3mg cholesterol, 255mg sodium.

Brie and Chutney Skins

Prepare potato skins as directed through step 2. Top skins with **3 table-spoons chopped jarred chutney**, then **2 ounces Brie cheese**, cut into 1/4-inch pieces. Sprinkle with **1/3 cup chopped pecans**. Bake until cheese melts, about 5 minutes.

Each potato skin: About 80 calories, 2g protein, 12g carbohydrate, 3g total fat (1g saturated), 2g fiber, 4mg cholesterol, 180mg sodium.

Potato Skins

Caviar in Potato Nests

A feast for the eyes as well as the palate, these may be the most luxurious appetizers you will ever serve. The potato nests can be baked up to four hours ahead. Let stand at room temperature on a paper towel–lined cookie sheet, then reheat in a 375°F oven.

PREP: 40 MINUTES PLUS CHILLING AND COOLING   BAKE: 25 MINUTES
MAKES 32 APPETIZERS

2 large baking potatoes (1¹/₂ pounds), not peeled, scrubbed
¹/₂ teaspoon salt
¹/₈ teaspoon ground black pepper

¹/₂ cup sour cream, at room temperature
1 ounce sevruga, osetra, salmon, or lumpfish caviar

1. In 3-quart saucepan, combine potatoes and enough *cold water* to cover; heat to boiling over high heat. Reduce heat; cover and simmer until tender, about 20 minutes. Drain potatoes; refrigerate until chilled, about 1 hour.

2. Preheat oven to 425°F. Grease thirty-two 1³/₄-inch mini muffin-pan cups. Peel and coarsely grate potatoes. Transfer to bowl and toss gently with salt and pepper.

3. Place about 1 heaping tablespoon potato mixture in each muffin-pan cup and press against bottom and up side as high as possible. Bake until edges of potato nests are golden brown, 25 to 30 minutes. Cool in pans on wire racks 10 minutes.

4. To serve, transfer warm potato nests to warm platter. Spoon 1 teaspoon sour cream into each nest and top with about ¹/₄ teaspoon caviar.

Each appetizer: About 26 calories, 1g protein, 3g carbohydrate, 1g total fat (1g saturated), 0g fiber, 7mg cholesterol, 52mg sodium.

Sweet and Spicy Nuts

PREP: 15 MINUTES PLUS COOLING   BAKE: ABOUT 25 MINUTES
MAKES ABOUT 8 CUPS

1 cup sugar
2 teaspoons salt
1 teaspoon ground cumin
1 teaspoon ground cinnamon
1 teaspoon coarsely ground black
  pepper

1/2 teaspoon ground red pepper
  (cayenne)
1 large egg white
6 cups unsalted nuts, such as
  walnuts, pecans, natural almonds,
  and/or cashews

1. Preheat oven to 325°F. Grease two 15 1/2" by 10 1/2" jelly-roll pans.

2. In small bowl, stir sugar, salt, cumin, cinnamon, black pepper, and red pepper. In large bowl, whisk egg white until foamy. Stir nuts into egg white. Add sugar mixture; toss until nuts are thoroughly coated.

3. Divide nut mixture between prepared pans, spreading evenly. Bake nuts until golden brown and dry, stirring twice during baking, 25 to 27 minutes. With slotted spoon, transfer nuts to waxed paper; spread in single layer to cool. Store nuts in tightly covered container at room temperature up to 1 month.

Each 1/4 cup: About 165 calories, 4g protein, 11g carbohydrate, 12g total fat (2g saturated), 2g fiber, 0mg cholesterol, 150mg sodium.

Microwave Spiced Popcorn

Our testers found this popcorn spicy but addictive! If you prefer a milder taste, use one teaspoon or less of hot sauce.

Microwave/Bake: 13 minutes   Makes about 5 cups

1 bag (3 1/2 ounces) natural flavor
  microwave popcorn
2 tablespoons butter or margarine

2 tablespoons spicy brown mustard
2 teaspoons chili powder
2 teaspoons hot pepper sauce

1. Preheat oven to 375°F.

2. Pop popcorn in microwave oven as label directs. (You should have about 8 cups popped corn.)

3. In large microwave-safe bowl, combine butter, mustard, chili powder, and hot pepper sauce. Cook, uncovered, in microwave oven on High 45 seconds, or until butter melts, stirring once.

4. Add popped corn to butter mixture and toss until well coated. Spread popcorn evenly into 15 1/2" by 10 1/2" jelly-roll pan. Bake until popcorn coating browns, 8 to 10 minutes. Cool completely in pan on wire rack. If not serving right away, store in large zip-tight plastic bag up to 3 days.

Each 1/2 cup: About 74 calories, 1g protein, 6g carbohydrate, 5g total fat (2g saturated), 1g fiber, 6mg cholesterol, 157mg sodium.

Firecracker Party Mix

In 1955, the home economists at Ralston Purina's Checkerboard Square in St. Louis created a party snack using Chex cereal squares. They tossed the cereal with pretzel sticks, nuts, and a spicy butter spiked with Worcestershire sauce. Over the years, numerous variations have evolved. This one mirrors the original recipe with one homemade touch: the nuts have been replaced with popped corn.

PREP: 10 MINUTES PLUS COOLING   BAKE: 30 MINUTES PER BATCH
MAKES ABOUT 25 CUPS

1/4 cup Worcestershire sauce
4 tablespoons butter or margarine
2 tablespoons brown sugar
1 1/2 teaspoons salt
1/2 to 1 teaspoon ground red pepper (cayenne)

12 cups popped corn (about 1/3 cup unpopped)
1 package (12 ounces) oven-toasted corn cereal squares
1 package (8 to 10 ounces) thin pretzel sticks

1. Preheat oven to 300°F. In 1-quart saucepan, combine Worcestershire, butter, brown sugar, salt, and ground red pepper; heat over low heat, stirring frequently, until butter has melted.

2. Place half each of popped corn, cereal, and pretzels in large roasting pan; toss with half of Worcestershire-butter mixture.

3. Bake popcorn mixture 30 minutes, stirring once halfway through baking. Cool mixture in very large bowl or on surface covered with waxed paper. Repeat with remaining popped corn, cereal, and pretzels and Worcestershire-butter mixture.

Each 1/2 cup: About 65 calories, 1g protein, 13g carbohydrate, 1g total fat (0g saturated), 1g fiber, 0mg cholesterol, 245mg sodium.

Hot and Sweet Nut Brittle

An addictive treat with a hot and spicy kick your friends will love!

PREP: 20 MINUTES   COOK: 30 MINUTES   MAKES ABOUT 1 3/4 POUNDS

1 pound blanched whole almonds	2 teaspoons ground cumin
2 cups plus 1 tablespoon sugar	1 teaspoon ground coriander
1/4 cup cider vinegar	1/2 to 3/4 teaspoon ground red pepper
2 teaspoons salt	(cayenne)

1. Preheat oven to 375°F. Lightly grease large cookie sheet. Place almonds in 15 1/2" by 10 1/2" jelly-roll pan. Bake, shaking pan occasionally, until golden brown, 10 to 15 minutes. Cool almonds in pan on wire rack.

2. While almonds are cooling, in heavy 3-quart saucepan, combine 2 cups sugar and vinegar; heat to boiling over medium heat. Continue cooking, stirring occasionally, until mixture turns dark amber in color, 15 to 20 minutes. If using a thermometer, temperature should reach about 360°F.

3. Meanwhile, in small bowl, combine salt, cumin, coriander, ground red pepper, and remaining 1 tablespoon sugar.

4. Remove saucepan from heat. Stir spice mixture into hot sugar syrup. Add almonds and stir until evenly coated. Immediately pour mixture on prepared cookie sheet. With 2 forks, spread almond mixture to form single layer.

5. Cool brittle completely on cookie sheet on wire rack. With hands, break brittle into small pieces. Store in airtight container up to 1 month.

Each ounce: About 145 calories, 4g protein, 18g carbohydrate, 8g total fat (1g saturated), 2g fiber, 0mg cholesterol, 155mg sodium.

Homemade Sushi

Bet you never thought you could learn to be a sushi chef at home! All our suggestions use cooked fish, such as shrimp or smoked salmon, and/or vegetables. And you can make the sushi rolls up to 6 hours before serving.

PREP: 1 1/2 HOURS PLUS CHILLING   COOK: 25 MINUTES
MAKES ABOUT 100 PIECES

FILLINGS

4 ounces cooked shrimp shelled and deveined, thinly sliced lengthwise

4 ounces imitation crab sticks (surimi), cut lengthwise into pencil-thin sticks

4 ounces thinly sliced smoked salmon

1 medium-ripe avocado, cut lengthwise in half, then thinly sliced lengthwise

1 carrot, cut crosswise in half, then lengthwise into 3" by 1/2" strips

1 small cucumber, cut lengthwise into 3" by 1/2" strips

GARNISHES

black sesame seeds

white sesame seeds, toasted

minced fresh chives plus whole chives

ACCOMPANIMENTS

pickled ginger

soy sauce

wasabi (Japanese horseradish)

SUSHI RICE

2 1/2 cups water

2 cups Japanese short-grain rice

2 tablespoons sugar

1 teaspoon salt

1/2 cup seasoned rice vinegar

1 package (ten 8" by 7" sheets) roasted seaweed for sushi (nori)*

1. Assemble fillings: In separate small bowls or dishes, place shrimp, crab sticks, smoked salmon, avocado, carrot, and cucumber. Cover bowls with plastic wrap and place in 15 1/2" by 10 1/2" jelly-roll pan for easier handling. Place in refrigerator until ready to use.

2. Assemble garnishes: In separate small bowls, place black sesame seeds, white sesame seeds, and minced chives.

3. Assemble accompaniments: In separate small serving dishes, place pickled ginger, soy sauce, and wasabi. Cover with plastic wrap and refrigerate.

Homemade Sushi

4. Prepare sushi rice: In 3-quart saucepan, combine water, rice, sugar, and salt; heat to boiling over high heat. Reduce heat to low; cover and simmer until rice is tender and liquid has been absorbed (rice will be sticky), about 25 minutes. Remove from heat; stir in vinegar. Cover and keep warm.

5. Make sushi rolls: Place 12-inch-long piece of plastic wrap on surface. Place small bowl of water nearby (it's easier to handle sticky rice with damp hands). Place 1 nori sheet, shiny (smooth) side down, on plastic wrap, with a short side facing you. Top with generous 1/2 cup rice. With small metal spatula and damp hands, spread and pat rice to make an even layer over nori, leaving 1/4-inch border all around. (To make an inside-out roll, flip rice-covered nori sheet over so that nori is on top.)

6. On top of rice (or nori), starting about 2 inches away from side nearest you, arrange desired fillings, placing them crosswise to form 1 1/2 inch-wide strip. Using end of plastic wrap closest to you, lift edge of sushi, then firmly roll sushi, jelly-roll fashion. Seal end of nori sheet with damp finger. (If making inside-out roll, coat outside of roll with one of the garnishes.) Place sushi roll on tray or platter.

7. Repeat to make 10 sushi rolls in all, replacing plastic wrap when necessary. Cover and refrigerate sushi rolls at least 30 minutes or up to 6 hours.

8. To serve, with serrated knife, slice off and discard ends from each sushi roll. Slice each roll crosswise into ten 1/2-inch-thick slices. Arrange sliced rolls, cut side up, on platter; garnish with whole chives. Serve with bowls of pickled ginger, soy sauce, and wasabi.

Each piece: About 25 calories, 1g protein, 4g carbohydrate, 0g total fat, 0g fiber, 3mg cholesterol, 70mg sodium.

★Sushi ingredients are available in specialty food stores and in the ethnic food sections of some supermarkets.

Mexican Meatballs

These tasty meatballs are simmered in a delicious tomato sauce that gets a hint of smoke from a chipotle chile in adobo, which is a smoked jalapeño chile in a vinegary marinade. Chipotle chiles are available in Hispanic markets and in some larger supermarkets.

PREP: 30 MINUTES   COOK: 45 MINUTES   MAKES 20 APPETIZER SERVINGS

1 1/2 pounds ground beef chuck
3/4 cup plain dried bread crumbs
1 large egg
3 garlic cloves, minced
1/4 cup water
1 1/4 teaspoons salt
1/2 teaspoon ground black pepper
1 can (28 ounces) plum tomatoes

1 chipotle chile in adobo
2 teaspoons vegetable oil
1 small onion, finely chopped
1 teaspoon ground cumin
1 cup chicken broth
1/4 cup coarsely chopped fresh
    cilantro

1. In large bowl, combine ground beef, bread crumbs, egg, one-third of garlic, water, 1 teaspoon salt, and pepper until blended but not over-mixed. With hands, shape into 3/4-inch meatballs, handling meat as little as possible.

2. In blender at low speed, blend tomatoes with their juice and chipotle chile until smooth.

3. In 5-quart Dutch oven, heat oil over medium heat. Add onion and cook, stirring frequently, until tender, about 5 minutes. Stir in cumin and remaining garlic; cook 30 seconds. Stir in tomato mixture, broth, and remaining 1/4 teaspoon salt; heat to boiling over high heat.

4. Add meatballs and heat to boiling. Reduce heat to low; simmer 30 minutes. Transfer meatballs and tomato mixture to chafing dish and sprinkle with cilantro.

Each serving: About 125 calories, 8g protein, 5g carbohydrate, 8g total fat (3g saturated), 1g fiber, 31mg cholesterol, 310mg sodium.

Mini Greek Meatballs

PREP: 25 MINUTES BROIL: 6 MINUTES MAKES 12 APPETIZER SERVINGS

1 tablespoon olive oil
1 small onion, finely chopped
2 garlic cloves, finely chopped
1 teaspoon ground cumin
1/8 teaspoon ground cinnamon
1 pound ground lamb or beef
1/2 cup fresh bread crumbs (about 1
   slice bread)
1 large egg, lightly beaten
2 tablespoons chopped fresh mint

1 tablespoon fresh lemon juice
3/4 teaspoon salt
1/4 teaspoon ground black pepper

YOGURT SAUCE
1 container (8 ounces) plain low-fat
   yogurt
2 green onions, finely chopped
1/8 teaspoon salt

1. Preheat broiler. Line broiling pan (without rack) with foil; spray with nonstick cooking spray.

2. Prepare meatballs: In 10-inch skillet, heat oil over medium heat. Add onion and garlic and cook, stirring occasionally, until tender, about 5 minutes. Stir in cumin and cinnamon. Transfer onion mixture to large bowl; cool slightly.

3. Add ground lamb, bread crumbs, egg, mint, lemon juice, salt, and pepper to onion mixture in bowl; mix just until well blended but not over-mixed. Shape into 1-inch meatballs, handling meat as little as possible. Place in prepared broiling pan. Place pan in broiler about 5 to 6 inches from heat source. Broil meatballs until cooked through, about 6 minutes.

4. Meanwhile, prepare Yogurt Sauce: In small serving bowl, combine yogurt, green onions, and salt.

5. Transfer meatballs to platter. Serve with sauce.

Each serving meatballs: About 105 calories, 8g protein, 2g carbohydrate, 7g total fat (3g saturated), 0g fiber, 45mg cholesterol, 185mg sodium.

Each tablespoon sauce: About 10 calories, 1g protein, 1g carbohydrate, 0g total fat, 0g fiber, 1mg cholesterol, 30mg sodium.

Mini Corn Dogs

It was over 60 years ago at the Texas State Fair that Neil Fletcher invented the "corny dog," a sausage on a stick, dipped in corn-bread batter and fried. This oven-baked version is a treat for kids of all ages.

PREP: 45 MINUTES BAKE: 15 MINUTES MAKES ABOUT 48 CORN DOGS

1²/₃ cups all-purpose flour
¹/₃ cup yellow cornmeal
1 tablespoon baking powder
1 teaspoon salt
3 tablespoons cold butter or
    margarine, cut into pieces
1 tablespoon shortening

³/₄ cup milk
1 package (16 ounces) miniature
    frankfurters (about 48), drained
    and patted dry
ketchup (optional)
mustard (optional)

1. In large bowl, combine flour, cornmeal, baking powder, and salt. With pastry blender or two knives used scissor-fashion, cut in butter and shortening until mixture resembles coarse crumbs. Stir in milk until mixture forms soft dough that leaves side of bowl.

2. Turn dough onto lightly floured surface; knead gently 4 to 5 times, just until smooth. With floured rolling pin, roll dough into 14-inch round (about ¹/₈ inch thick).

3. Preheat oven to 450°F. With floured 2¹/₄-inch biscuit cutter, cut out as many rounds as possible. Press trimmings together; wrap in plastic wrap and set aside. Place 1 frankfurter on each dough round. Bring sides of dough up around frankfurter; pinch in center to seal. Place wrapped frankfurters, seam side up, 1¹/₂ inches apart, on ungreased large cookie sheet.

4. Bake corn dogs until biscuits are golden, 12 to 15 minutes. Repeat with remaining frankfurters and dough. Press together dough trimmings and reroll.

5. Serve warm with ketchup and mustard, if you like.

Each corn dog: About 60 calories, 2g protein, 5g carbohydrate, 4g total fat (1g saturated), 0g fiber, 6mg cholesterol, 180mg sodium.

Mini Corn Dogs

Empanaditas

These two-bite savory pastries are stuffed with picadillo, a spiced ground beef mixture that is delicately sweetened with raisins.

PREP: 1 HOUR 15 MINUTES BAKE: 12 MINUTES PER BATCH
MAKES ABOUT 54 TURNOVERS

FLAKY PASTRY
3 cups all-purpose flour
1 1/2 teaspoons baking powder
3/4 teaspoon salt
1 cup vegetable shortening
about 6 tablespoons ice water

FILLING
2 teaspoons vegetable oil
1 small onion, finely chopped
1 large garlic clove, finely chopped
1/4 teaspoon ground cinnamon

1/4 teaspoon ground red pepper
(cayenne)
4 ounces ground beef chuck
1/4 teaspoon salt
1 cup canned tomatoes with their
juice
3 tablespoons chopped golden raisins
3 tablespoons chopped pimiento-
stuffed olives (salad olives)
1 large egg beaten with 2
tablespoons water

1. Prepare Flaky Turnover Pastry. In large bowl, combine flour, baking powder, and salt. With pastry blender or two knives used scissor-fashion, cut in shortening until mixture resembles coarse crumbs. Sprinkle in ice water, 1 tablespoon at a time, mixing with fork after each addition, until dough is just moist enough to hold together. Shape into ball. Wrap in waxed paper and refrigerate while preparing filling or up to overnight.

2. Prepare filling: In 10-inch skillet, heat oil over medium heat. Add onion and cook, stirring frequently, until tender, about 5 minutes. Stir in garlic, cinnamon, and ground red pepper; cook 30 seconds. Increase heat to medium-high; add ground beef and salt and cook, stirring frequently, until beef begins to brown, about 5 minutes. Stir in tomatoes with their juice, raisins, and olives, breaking up tomatoes with side of spoon; cook over high heat until liquid has almost evaporated, 7 to 10 minutes. Remove from heat.

3. Preheat oven to 425°F. Divide dough into 4 equal pieces. On floured surface, with floured rolling pin, roll 1 piece of dough 1/16 inch thick. Keep remaining dough covered. With 3-inch biscuit cutter, cut out as many rounds as possible, reserving trimmings. On one half of each dough round, place 1 level teaspoon filling. Brush edges of rounds with some beaten egg mixture. Fold dough over to enclose filling. With fork, press edges together to seal dough; prick top. Brush turnovers lightly with some egg mixture. With spatula, lift turnovers and arrange 1 inch apart on ungreased large cookie sheet.

4. Bake turnovers until just golden, 12 to 15 minutes. Repeat with remaining dough, filling, and egg mixture. Press together dough trimmings and reroll. Serve hot or warm.

Each turnover: About 72 calories, 1g protein, 6g carbohydrate, 5g total fat (1g saturated), 0g fiber, 6mg cholesterol, 78mg sodium.

Lacy Parmesan Crisps

PREP: 20 MINUTES   BAKE: 6 MINUTES PER BATCH
MAKES ABOUT 24 CRISPS

1¹/₂ cups coarsely grated Parmesan cheese (6 ounces)

1. Preheat oven to 375°F. Line large cookie sheet with reusable nonstick bakeware liner. Spoon Parmesan by level tablespoons, about 3 inches apart, on prepared cookie sheet. Spread each mound into 2-inch round.

2. Bake cheese rounds until edges just begin to color, 6 to 7 minutes. Transfer bakeware liner to wire rack; cool 2 minutes. Transfer crisps to paper towels. Repeat with remaining cheese. If not serving right away, store crisps in airtight container up to 4 days. Reheat in a 375°F oven for 3 mintues to serve warm.

Each crisp: About 30 calories, 3g protein, 0g carbohydrate, 2g total fat (1g saturated), 0g fiber, 6mg cholesterol, 130mg sodium.

Greek Cheese Pastries

A peppery feta-ricotta cheese filling and store-bought phyllo are transformed into easy-to-make treats.

PREP: 1 HOUR 15 MINUTES BAKE: 15 MINUTES MAKES 75 APPETIZERS

1 package (8 ounces) feta cheese, well drained and crumbled
1 cup part-skim ricotta cheese
2 large eggs
1/4 cup chopped fresh parsley
1/2 teaspoon coarsely ground black pepper
15 sheets (16" by 12" each) fresh or frozen (thawed) phyllo
1/2 cup butter or margarine (1 stick), melted

1. Grease two 15 1/2" by 10 1/2" jelly-roll pans. In medium bowl, with fork, finely crumble feta; stir in ricotta, eggs, parsley, and pepper.

2. On surface, stack 5 phyllo sheets and cut lengthwise into 5 equal strips. Place cut phyllo on waxed paper; cover completely to prevent it from drying out. Place 1 phyllo strip on surface; brush with some melted butter. Place 1 rounded teaspoon filling at end of strip. Fold one corner of strip diagonally over filling. Continue folding over at right angles to end of strip. Repeat filling and shaping with remaining phyllo and filling, placing triangles about 1 inch apart in prepared pans. Brush with melted butter.

3. If not serving right away, cover and refrigerate up to several hours. Or to freeze, prepare as directed but do not bake. Freeze in jelly-roll pans, then store in freezer in airtight containers between layers of waxed paper up to 1 month.

4. Preheat oven to 400°F. Bake pastries until golden, 15 to 20 minutes.

Each appetizer: About 37 calories, 1g protein, 2g carbohydrate, 3g total fat (1g saturated), 0g fiber, 13mg cholesterol, 70mg sodium.

Curried Cheddar Puffs

A hot blend of curry powder, coriander, and cumin adds exotic flavor to these hard-to-resist morsels. Bake and freeze the puffs up to a month ahead so they're ready for company when you are.

PREP: 20 MINUTES BAKE: 25 MINUTES MAKES ABOUT 96 PUFFS

2 teaspoons curry powder
1/2 teaspoon ground coriander
1/2 teaspoon ground cumin
1/4 teaspoon ground red pepper
  (cayenne)
1 cup water
6 tablespoons butter or margarine,
  cut into pieces

1/2 teaspoon salt
1 cup all-purpose flour
4 large eggs
4 ounces Cheddar cheese, shredded
  (1 cup)

1. Preheat oven to 400°F. Grease 2 large cookie sheets.

2. In 3-quart saucepan, combine curry powder, coriander, cumin, and ground red pepper. Heat over medium heat, stirring constantly, until very fragrant, about 1 minute. Stir in water, butter, and salt; heat to boiling over high heat. Remove from heat. With wooden spoon, stir in flour all at once. Return pan to medium-low heat, stirring constantly, until mixture forms a ball and leaves side of pan. Remove from heat.

3. Stir in eggs, one at a time, beating well after each addition until batter is smooth and satiny. Stir in Cheddar. Spoon batter into large pastry bag fitted with 1/2-inch plain tip. Pipe batter, about 1 inch apart, on prepared cookie sheets, forming 1-inch-wide and 3/4-inch-high mounds. (Or, drop dough by teaspoons, forming small mounds.) With fingertip dipped in cool water, gently smooth peaks.

4. Bake puffs until deep golden, 25 to 30 minutes, rotating cookie sheets between upper and lower racks halfway through baking. Transfer to wire racks to cool. Repeat with remaining batter.

5. Serve puffs at room temperature or reheat in 400°F oven 5 minutes to serve warm.

Each puff: About 20 calories, 1g protein, 1g carbohydrate, 1g total fat (1g saturated), 0g fiber, 12mg cholesterol, 28mg sodium.

Brie in Puff Pastry

The perfect combination of rich, ripened Brie encased in a flaky pastry crust.

PREP: 20 MINUTES   BAKE: 30 MINUTES   MAKES 24 SERVINGS

1 package (17 1/4 ounces) frozen puff pastry sheets, thawed
1 wheel (8 inches in diameter) Brie cheese (2 pounds)
1 large egg yolk beaten with 1 tablespoon water
green and red seedless grape clusters

1. Preheat oven to 425°F. On lightly floured surface, unfold 1 sheet puff pastry. With floured rolling pin, roll dough into 13" by 10" rectangle. Cut 13" by 1 1/2" strip and 8 1/2" round from rectangle. Repeat with remaining sheet puff pastry.

2. Place 1 pastry round on ungreased cookie sheet; center Brie on pastry. Brush side of Brie with some egg-yolk mixture. Wrap 2 long pastry strips around side of Brie; press strips firmly against Brie to keep in place. Brush pastry strips with some yolk mixture.

3. Place second pastry round on top of Brie. Press edges of rounds to pastry strips to seal Brie completely in pastry. With tip of knife, score top of pastry into 1-inch squares. Brush top and side of pastry with remaining yolk mixture. Bake until pastry is golden brown, 30 to 35 minutes.

4. Let Brie stand at room temperature about 2 hours, to firm slightly.

5. To serve, with 1 or 2 spatulas, transfer Brie to large deep platter. Decorate with small clusters of grapes. Place a knife alongside for cutting the pastry-wrapped Brie into serving pieces.

Each serving: About 244 calories, 9g protein, 10g carbohydrate, 19g total fat (8g saturated), 0g fiber, 47mg cholesterol, 290mg sodium.

Stilton and Apple Napoleons

These miniature Napoleons showcase the classic flavor combination of Stilton and apple. You can make the apple puree, the Stilton mixture, and also bake the pastry a day ahead. To prevent it from getting soggy, assemble the napoleons just a few hours before serving.

PREP: 30 MINUTES BAKE: 20 MINUTES MAKES ABOUT 36 NAPOLEONS

1 sheet frozen puff pastry (half 17 1/4-ounce package), thawed

3 tablespoons unsalted butter or margarine, softened

2 large Golden Delicious apples, peeled, cored, and chopped

2 1/2 ounces Stilton cheese, softened (1/3 cup)

1/4 cup walnuts, toasted and finely chopped

1 tablespoon chopped fresh parsley

1. Preheat oven to 400°F. On lightly floured surface, unfold puff pastry. With floured rolling pin, roll dough to 17" by 13" rectangle. Transfer to ungreased large cookie sheet. Using ruler as guide, cut pastry lengthwise into six 17" by 2" strips. Discard trimmings. Place second cookie sheet on top of pastry.

2. Bake until pastry is golden, 17 to 20 minutes. Cool on cookie sheet on wire rack.

3. In 10-inch skillet, melt 1 tablespoon butter over medium heat. Stir in apples; cover and cook until tender and beginning to brown, 10 to 15 minutes. Remove from heat; mash with back of spoon.

4. In small bowl, stir cheese and remaining 2 tablespoons butter until blended. Stir in walnuts and parsley.

5. Spread cheese mixture evenly on 2 pastry strips. Spread apple mixture evenly on another 2 pastry strips. Stack apple layers on cheese layers; top with remaining 2 pastry strips. With serrated knife, trim ends and cut pastry crosswise into 3/4-inch-wide slices.

Each napoleon: About 100 calories, 2g protein, 7g carbohydrate, 7g total fat (2g saturated), 0g fiber, 4mg cholesterol, 62mg sodium.

Asparagus, Gruyère and Mushroom Strudel

You can prepare this strudel early in the day. Refrigerate the unbaked packets covered with plastic. Just pop into the oven twenty-five minutes before serving.

PREP: 40 MINUTES BAKE: 25 MINUTES MAKES 6 FIRST-COURSE SERVINGS

24 asparagus spears (about 1 1/4 pounds)
1 teaspoon salt
4 tablespoons butter or margarine
1 pound white mushrooms, trimmed and thinly sliced
2 teaspoons fresh lemon juice
1/3 cup walnuts, toasted and finely chopped

3 tablespoons plain dried bread crumbs
12 sheets (16" by 12" each) fresh or frozen (thawed) phyllo
3 ounces Gruyère or Swiss cheese, shredded (3/4 cup)

1. Cut asparagus into 6-inch-long spears (reserve ends for soup or discard). In nonstick 12-inch skillet, heat *1/2 inch water* to boiling over high heat. Add asparagus and 1/2 teaspoon salt; heat to boiling. Reduce heat to medium low; cook until asparagus is tender, 4 to 8 minutes; drain. Wipe skillet dry.

2. In same skillet, melt 1 tablespoon butter over medium-high heat. Add mushrooms and remaining 1/2 teaspoon salt; cook until mushrooms have browned and liquid has evaporated. Add lemon juice; cook 30 seconds. Transfer mushrooms to plate to cool slightly.

3. Preheat oven to 375°F. Lightly grease large cookie sheet. Melt remaining 3 tablespoons butter. In small bowl, toss walnuts and bread crumbs until combined.

4. On surface, place 1 phyllo sheet with short side facing you; brush lightly with some melted butter. Sprinkle with one-sixth of walnut mixture. Top with another phyllo sheet; lightly brush with butter, being careful not to tear phyllo. Sprinkle one-sixth of Gruyère on phyllo, leaving 2-inch border on short side facing you and 1 1/2-inch borders on two

longer sides. Place 3 asparagus spears, side by side, on cheese; top with one-sixth of mushrooms. Roll up phyllo, jelly-roll fashion, just enough to enclose filling. Fold both sides of phyllo in toward center, then continue rolling phyllo to end. Place packet, seam side down, on prepared cookie sheet. Brush packet lightly with some butter. Repeat to make 5 more packets.

5. Bake packets until slightly puffed and golden brown, about 25 minutes. Serve hot or warm.

Each serving: About 334 calories, 12g protein, 30g carbohydrate, 20g total fat (4g saturated), 4g fiber, 36mg cholesterol, 580mg sodium.

Green-Onion Purses with Yogurt Sauce

Green-Onion Purses with Yogurt Sauce

Wonton based appetizers are impressive, yet surprisingly easy to put together.

PREP: 20 MINUTES   COOK: 4 MINUTES PER BATCH
MAKES ABOUT 24 DUMPLINGS

2 tablespoons butter or margarine
3 bunches green onions, chopped
1/8 teaspoon coarsely ground black
 pepper
2 1/2 teaspoons salt
1 container (8 ounces) plain low-fat
 yogurt

1 garlic clove, crushed with garlic
 press
1 tablespoon finely chopped fresh
 mint or cilantro
24 wonton wrappers (3 1/2" by 3 1/4"
 each, about half 12-ounce
 package)

1. Dust jelly-roll pan with cornstarch or all-purpose flour. In 12-inch skillet, melt butter over medium heat. Add green onions, pepper, and 1/4 teaspoon salt. Cook green onions, stirring occasionally, until soft but not browned, 8 to 10 minutes. Remove from heat; cool 10 minutes.

2. Meanwhile, in 5-quart saucepot, heat *3 quarts water* and 2 teaspoons salt to boiling over high heat.

3. In small bowl, combine yogurt, garlic, mint, and 1/4 teaspoon salt.

4. Arrange 8 wonton wrappers on surface. Place 1 rounded teaspoon green onion filling in center of each wrapper. Run dampened finger around edge of wontons to moisten, rewetting fingers as necessary. Fold each wonton wrapper on diagonal over filling to form a triangle. Pinch and pleat edges of dumpling to seal in filling.

5. Place dumplings in prepared pan. Cover dumplings with damp (not wet) paper towels to prevent them from drying out.

6. Repeat with remaining filling and wonton skins to make about 24 dumplings in all.

7. Cook dumplings, in two batches, in boiling water, until cooked through, 4 to 5 minutes. With slotted spoon, transfer dumplings to platter. Repeat with remaining dumplings. Serve with yogurt sauce.

Each dumpling with sauce: About 40 calories, 1g protein, 6g carbohydrate, 1g total fat (0g saturated), 0g fiber, 4mg cholesterol, 295mg sodium.

Chinese Dumplings

Steamed dumplings are fun to make at home. Have them for brunch: it's the classic Chinese way to enjoy them.

PREP: 45 MINUTES   COOK: 10 MINUTES   MAKES 36 DUMPLINGS

2 cups tightly packed sliced napa cabbage (Chinese cabbage)
8 ounces ground pork
1 green onion, finely chopped
1½ teaspoons minced, peeled fresh ginger

2 tablespoons soy sauce
1 tablespoon dry sherry
2 teaspoons cornstarch
36 wonton wrappers (9 ounces)
1 large egg white, beaten
Soy Dipping Sauce (page 49)

1. Prepare filling: In 2-quart saucepan, heat *1 inch water* to boiling over high heat. Add cabbage and heat to boiling. Cook 1 minute; drain. Immediately rinse with cold running water to stop cooking. With hands, squeeze out as much water from cabbage as possible. Finely chop cabbage. Squeeze out any remaining water from cabbage; place in medium bowl. Stir in ground pork, green onion, ginger, soy sauce, sherry, and cornstarch until well blended.

2. Arrange half of wonton wrappers on waxed paper. With pastry brush, brush each wrapper lightly with egg white. Spoon 1 rounded teaspoon filling in center of each wrapper. Bring two opposite corners of each wonton wrapper together over filling; pinch and pleat edges to seal in filling. Repeat with remaining wrappers, egg white, and filling.

3. In deep nonstick 12-inch skillet, heat *½ inch water* to boiling over high heat. Place all dumplings, pleated edges up, in one layer in skillet. With spatula, move dumplings gently to prevent them from sticking to bottom of skillet. Heat to boiling. Reduce heat; cover and simmer until dumplings are cooked through, about 5 minutes.

4. With slotted spoon, transfer dumplings to platter. Serve with Soy Dipping Sauce.

Each dumpling: About 40 calories, 2g protein, 5g carbohydrate, 1g total fat (1g saturated), 0g fiber, 5mg cholesterol, 103mg sodium.

Chinese Dumplings

Roasted Beef Tenderloin

The most tender of all cuts of beef—the tenderloin—makes a luscious centerpiece on a buffet table. Serve it with thinly sliced baguette, rye and pumpernickel. Set out a choice of sauces, if you like. Try Green Herb Sauce, page 55, Plum and Five-Spice Sauce, page 30, Tomato-Ginger Relish, page 33, or Margarita Mustard, page 30.

PREP: 20 MINUTES PLUS MARINATING   ROAST: 40 MINUTES
MAKES 40 APPETIZER SERVINGS

MARINADE & BEEF
2 cups dry red wine
2 tablespoons olive oil
1 medium onion, sliced
1 tablespoon chopped fresh rosemary
  leaves
2 garlic cloves, crushed with garlic
  press
2 bay leaves
1 whole beef tenderloin trimmed
  (about 4 pounds),*
1/4 cup cracked black peppercorns

HORSERADISH-TARRAGON SAUCE
2/3 cup mayonnaise
1/2 cup sour cream
2 to 3 tablespoons chopped fresh
  tarragon leaves
2 tablespoons bottled white
  horseradish, drained
1 tablespoon Dijon mustard

assorted breads, thinly sliced

1. Prepare marinade: In jumbo (2-gallon) zip-tight plastic bag, combine red wine, oil, onion, rosemary, garlic, and bay leaves. Add tenderloin, turning to coat. Seal bag, pressing out as much air as possible. Place bag in shallow baking dish; refrigerate at least 4 hours or overnight, turning bag occasionally.

2. Preheat oven to 425°F. Remove meat from marinade; turn thinner end of meat under to make meat an even thickness. With string, tie tenderloin at 2-inch intervals to help hold its shape. Place peppercorns on waxed paper. Press tenderloin into peppercorns, turning to coat.

3. Place tenderloin on rack in large roasting pan (17" by 11 1/2"); roast until meat thermometer inserted in center of meat reaches 140°F, 40 to 45 minutes. Internal temperature of meat will rise to 145°F (medium) upon standing. Or roast until desired doneness. Transfer tenderloin to warm large platter; let stand 10 minutes to set juices for easier slicing.

4. Meanwhile, prepare horseradish-tarragon sauce: In small bowl, combine mayonnaise, sour cream, tarragon, horseradish, and mustard; stir until

well blended. Cover and refrigerate if not serving right away.
5. To serve, remove string and cut tenderloin into thin slices. Serve with assorted breads and horseradish-tarragon sauce.

Each serving with sauce: About 122 calories, 11g protein, 1g carbohydrate, 8g total fat (2g saturated), 0g fiber, 35mg cholesterol, 63mg sodium.

*If you buy an untrimmed tenderloin, it should weigh 6 to 6 1/2 pounds to yield about 4 pounds trimmed.

Devils on Horseback

These are wonderfully rich. Use soft, plump pitted prunes and a smoky bacon for best flavor.

PREP: 12 MINUTES PLUS MARINATING BAKE: 7 MINUTES
MAKES 16 APPETIZERS

1/4 **cup port wine**	**8 thin slices bacon**
1 teaspoon Dijon mustard	**16 large pitted prunes**
1 teaspoon sugar	

1. In medium bowl, with wire whisk, whisk port, mustard, and sugar until blended. Cut bacon slices crosswise in half and wrap 1 piece around each prune. Secure with toothpicks.
2. Place bacon-wrapped prunes in bowl with port mixture and toss to coat. Cover and refrigerate at least 1 hour or up to overnight.
3. Preheat broiler. Place bacon-wrapped prunes on rack in broiling pan. Broil, 6 inches from heat source, turning once, until bacon is cooked and browned, 7 to 8 minutes.

Each appetizer: About 96 calories, 5g protein, 6g carbohydrate, 5g total fat (2g saturated), 1g fiber, 15mg cholesterol, 318mg sodium.

Bite-Size Bacon Quiches

You can omit the bacon and stir ¹/₄ cup freshly grated Parmesan into the filling instead.

PREP: 1 HOUR PLUS CHILLING   BAKE: 20 MINUTES   MAKES 36 QUICHES

PASTRY DOUGH
2¹/₄ cups all-purpose flour
¹/₂ teaspoon salt
¹/₂ cup cold butter or margarine
   (1 stick), cut into pieces
¹/₄ cup vegetable shortening
4 to 6 tablespoons ice water
1 tablespoon butter or margarine,
   melted

BACON FILLING
1 package (8 ounces) bacon, finely
   chopped
1 cup half-and-half or light cream
2 large eggs
¹/₄ teaspoon salt
3 ounces Swiss cheese, shredded
   (³/₄ cup)

1. Prepare pastry dough: In large bowl, combine flour and salt. With pastry blender or two knives used scissor-fashion, cut in butter and shortening until mixture resembles coarse crumbs. Sprinkle in ice water, 1 tablespoon at a time, mixing lightly with fork after each addition, until dough is just moist enough to hold together. Shape dough into two disks; wrap each disk in plastic wrap and refrigerate 30 minutes or up to overnight. (If chilled overnight, let stand 30 minutes at room temperature before rolling.)

2. Grease and flour thirty-six 1³/₄-inch mini muffin-pan cups. On lightly floured surface, with floured rolling pin, roll dough until ¹/₈ inch thick. Using 3-inch fluted round cookie cutter, cut dough into 36 rounds, rerolling trimmings.

3. Preheat oven to 400°F. Line muffin-pan cups with dough rounds; brush lightly with melted butter. Cover and refrigerate up to 1 day.

4. Prepare bacon filling: In 12-inch skillet, cook bacon over medium heat until browned. Transfer bacon to paper towels to drain.

5. In small bowl, beat half-and-half, eggs, and salt. Divide bacon and cheese among pastry cups. Spoon about 1 tablespoon egg mixture into each cup. Bake until knife inserted in center of quiche comes out clean, 20 to 25 minutes. Remove quiches from pan; serve hot.

Each quiche: About 111 calories, 3g protein, 7g carbohydrate, 8g total fat (4g saturated), 0g fiber, 26mg cholesterol, 118mg sodium.

Stuffed Eggs

Stuffed eggs are make-ahead appetizers that are perfect for a crowd. Cook a couple of dozen eggs and try all our simple variations!

PREP: 30 MINUTES COOK: 10 MINUTES PLUS STANDING
MAKES 12 APPETIZERS

6 large eggs	**1 tablespoon milk**
¼ cup mayonnaise	**⅛ teaspoon salt**

1. In 3-quart saucepan, place eggs and enough *cold water* to cover by at least 1 inch; heat to boiling over high heat. Immediately remove from heat and cover tightly; let stand 15 minutes. Pour off hot water and run cold water over eggs to cool. Peel eggs.

2. Slice eggs lengthwise in half. Gently remove yolks and place in small bowl; with fork, finely mash yolks. Stir in mayonnaise, milk, and salt until evenly blended. Egg-yolk mixture and egg whites can be covered separately and refrigerated up to 24 hours.

3. Place egg whites in jelly-roll pan lined with paper towels (to prevent eggs from rolling). Spoon egg-yolk mixture into pastry bag fitted with star tip or zip-tight plastic bag with one corner cut off. Pipe about 1 tablespoon yolk mixture into each egg-white half, or spoon in egg mixture. Cover eggs and refrigerate up to 4 hours.

Each appetizer: About 72 calories, 3g protein, 0g carbohydrate, 6g total fat (1g saturated), 0g fiber, 109mg cholesterol, 82mg sodium.

Bacon-Horseradish Stuffed Eggs

Prepare as directed but add **2 tablespoons crumbled crisp-cooked bacon** and **1 tablespoon bottled white horseradish** to yolk mixture. If not serving right away, sprinkle crumbled bacon on top of stuffed eggs instead of adding to yolk mixture.

Each appetizer: About 80 calories, 4g protein, 1g carbohydrate, 7g total fat (2g saturated), 0g fiber, 110mg cholesterol, 102mg sodium.

Lemon-Basil Stuffed Eggs

Dried Tomato–Caper Stuffed Eggs

Prepare as directed but add **1 tablespoon plus 2 teaspoons chopped dried tomatoes packed in oil and herbs**, **1 tablespoon plus 2 teaspoons chopped drained capers**, and **1/8 teaspoon coarsely ground black pepper** to yolk mixture.

Each appetizer: About 78 calories, 3g protein, 1g carbohydrate, 7g total fat (1g saturated), 0g fiber, 109mg cholesterol, 143mg sodium.

Lemon-Basil Stuffed Eggs

Prepare as directed but add **1 tablespoon chopped fresh basil**, **1/4 teaspoon freshly grated lemon peel**, and **1/4 teaspoon coarsely ground black pepper** to yolk mixture.

Each appetizer: About 73 calories, 3g protein, 0g carbohydrate, 6g total fat (1g saturated), 0g fiber, 109mg cholesterol, 82mg sodium.

Pimiento-Studded Stuffed Eggs

Prepare as directed but add **2 tablespoons chopped pimientos**, **2 teaspoons Dijon mustard**, and **1/8 teaspoon ground red pepper (cayenne)** to yolk mixture.

Each appetizer: About 74 calories, 3g protein, 1g carbohydrate, 6g total fat (1g saturated), 0g fiber, 109mg cholesterol, 102mg sodium.

Omelet Española Squares

Our potato omelet is a variation on one of Spain's most popular tapas, which is called a tortilla in Spain. It tastes best when made ahead and served at room temperature. Garnish with fresh chives.

PREP: 45 MINUTES   BAKE: 15 MINUTES   MAKES ABOUT 60 APPETIZERS

2 tablespoons olive oil
1 pound all-purpose potatoes
   (3 medium), scrubbed and cut
   into 1/4-inch pieces
1 medium onion, sliced
1 medium green pepper, chopped
3/4 teaspoon salt
8 large eggs

1/2 cup water
1/4 teaspoon coarsely ground black
   pepper
1 can (14 1/2 to 16 ounces) diced
   tomatoes, drained
1/2 cup chopped pimiento-stuffed
   olives (salad olives)

1. In nonstick 10-inch oven-safe skillet, (if skillet is not oven-safe, wrap handle with double layer of foil), heat oil over medium heat. Add potatoes, onion, green pepper, and 1/4 teaspoon salt; cook, stirring occasionally, until vegetables are tender, about 20 minutes.

2. Meanwhile, preheat oven to 400°F. In medium bowl, with wire whisk or fork, beat eggs, water, remaining 1/2 teaspoon salt, and pepper. Stir in tomatoes and olives. Stir egg mixture into potato mixture in skillet; cook, covered, until egg mixture begins to set around edge, about 5 minutes. Remove cover and place skillet in oven; bake until omelet sets, 15 to 20 minutes.

3. Carefully invert omelet onto large flat plate. Cool; cut into 1-inch squares.

Each appetizer: About 28 calories, 1g protein, 2g carbohydrate, 1g total fat (0g saturated), 0g fiber, 28mg cholesterol, 63mg sodium.

Buffalo-Style Chicken Wings

Here's a broiled version of one of America's favorite appetizers. Serve with plenty of napkins!

PREP: 15 MINUTES   BROIL: 20 MINUTES   MAKES 18 APPETIZERS

4 ounces blue cheese, crumbled (1 cup)
1/2 cup sour cream
1/4 cup mayonnaise
1/4 cup milk
1/4 cup chopped fresh parsley
1 tablespoon fresh lemon juice

1/2 teaspoon salt
3 pounds chicken wings (18 wings), tips discarded, if desired
3 tablespoons butter or margarine
1/4 cup hot pepper sauce
1 medium bunch celery, cut into sticks

1. Preheat broiler. In medium bowl, combine blue cheese, sour cream, mayonnaise, milk, parsley, lemon juice, and 1/4 teaspoon salt. Cover and refrigerate.

2. Arrange chicken wings on rack in broiling pan; sprinkle with remaining 1/4 teaspoon salt. Broil 5 inches from heat source 10 minutes. Turn wings and broil until golden, 10 to 15 minutes longer.

3. Meanwhile, in small saucepan, melt butter with hot pepper sauce over low heat, stirring occasionally; keep hot.

4. In large bowl, toss wings with seasoned butter to coat on all sides. Arrange chicken wings and celery on platter along with blue-cheese sauce.

Each appetizer (without wingtip): About 169 calories, 10g protein, 3g carbohydrate, 13g total fat (5g saturated), 0g fiber, 39mg cholesterol, 349mg sodium.

Chicken and Beef Saté

Chicken and Beef Saté

PREP: 45 MINUTES PLUS MARINATING   GRILL: 3 MINUTES PER BATCH
MAKES 12 APPETIZER SERVINGS

1 pound skinless, boneless chicken-breast halves

1 boneless beef top sirloin steak, 1 inch thick (about 1¼ pounds)

2 large limes

¼ cup soy sauce

1 tablespoon grated, peeled fresh ginger

2 teaspoons sugar

2 garlic cloves, crushed with garlic press

24 (10-inch) wooden skewers

Spicy Peanut Sauce (page 172)

Cucumber Relish (page 172)

1. Cut chicken breasts lengthwise into ¾-inch-wide strips; place in medium bowl. Holding knife almost parallel to surface, slice steak crosswise into thin strips; place in separate bowl.

2. From limes, grate 2 teaspoons peel and squeeze 2 tablespoons juice. In small bowl, with wire whisk, mix lime peel and juice, soy sauce, ginger, sugar, and garlic. Stir half of soy-sauce mixture into beef. Stir remaining soy-sauce mixture into chicken. Cover bowls and refrigerate 30 minutes to marinate.

3. Meanwhile, prepare grill. Soak wooden skewers in water 20 minutes. Prepare Spicy Peanut Sauce and Cucumber Relish.

4. Thread chicken strips and beef strips, accordion-style, on separate wooden skewers.

5. Grill chicken and beef strips over medium heat, turning once, until just cooked through, 3 to 7 minutes. Pile skewers onto platter and serve with Spicy Peanut Sauce and Cucumber Relish.

Each serving without sauce or relish: About 125 calories, 20g protein, 1g carbohydrate, 4g total fat (2g saturated), 0g fiber, 52mg cholesterol, 218mg sodium.

Spicy Peanut Sauce

In medium bowl, with wire whisk or fork, mix $1/4$ **cup creamy peanut butter**, $1/4$ **cup very hot tap water**, **4 teaspoons seasoned rice vinegar**, **1 tablespoon soy sauce**, **1 tablespoon light (mild) molasses**, and $1/8$ **teaspoon crushed red pepper** until smooth. Makes about $2/3$ cup.

Each tablespoon: About 45 calories, 2g protein, 3g carbohydrate, 3g total fat (1g saturated), 1g fiber, 0mg cholesterol, 170mg sodium.

Cucumber Relish

In medium bowl, mix **4 medium Kirby cucumbers (about 4 ounces each)**, diced, $1/4$ **cup seasoned rice vinegar**, **2 tablespoons diced red onion**, **1 tablespoon vegetable oil**, and $1/4$ **teaspoon crushed red pepper**. Makes about $2 1/2$ cups.

Each $1/4$ cup: About 30 calories, 0g protein, 4g carbohydrate, 1g total fat (0g saturated), 1g fiber, 0mg cholesterol, 160mg sodium.

Shrimp Toast

PREP: 1 HOUR COOK: 1 MINUTE PER BATCH MAKES 48 SHRIMP TOASTS

1 pound small shrimp, shelled and deveined or 1 package (12 ounces) frozen shelled and deveined shrimp, thawed
1 large egg white
2 green onions, finely chopped
2 garlic cloves, crushed with garlic press
2 tablespoons grated, peeled fresh ginger
2 tablespoons dry sherry
2 tablespoons soy sauce
1 tablespoon cornstarch
1 teaspoon sugar
1/2 teaspoon Asian sesame oil
1/8 teaspoon ground black pepper
1/8 teaspoon ground red pepper (cayenne)
12 very thin slices white bread
1/2 cup plain dried bread crumbs
4 1/2 cups vegetable oil

1. If using frozen shrimp, drain very well. In blender or in food processor with knife blade attached, combine shrimp, egg white, green onions, garlic, ginger, sherry, soy sauce, cornstarch, sugar, sesame oil, and black and ground red peppers; puree until finely chopped.

2. Trim crusts from bread slices and cut each slice into 4 triangles. With a small metal spatula, spread 1 rounded teaspoonful shrimp mixture onto each triangle; scrape edges so filling will be neat. Dip shrimp side of each triangle into bread crumbs.

3. Meanwhile, in 4-quart saucepan, heat oil over medium heat until it reaches 360°F on deep-fat thermometer.

4. Place 4 to 5 triangles, shrimp side down, in slotted spoon, and carefully lower into hot oil. Cook until lightly browned, about 1 minute. Turn and cook until bread is golden, about 30 seconds longer. Transfer to paper towels to drain; keep warm. Repeat with remaining triangles. Serve hot. To reheat, place shrimp toast on ungreased cookie sheet; bake at 375°F for 8 to 10 minutes.

Each shrimp toast: About 218 calories, 3g protein, 5g carbohydrate, 22g total fat (3g saturated), 0g fiber, 14mg cholesterol, 126mg sodium.

Pickled Shrimp

Long a favorite in the *Good Housekeeping* dining room, this perfectly spiced appetizer is always made ahead: The shrimp are cooked the day before and marinated overnight. To keep them well chilled when served, set the bowl of shrimp in a larger bowl of crushed ice.

PREP: 20 MINUTES PLUS OVERNIGHT TO MARINATE   COOK: 5 MINUTES
MAKES 24 APPETIZER SERVINGS

1/4 cup dry sherry
3 teaspoons salt
1/4 teaspoon whole black peppercorns
1 bay leaf
3 pounds large shrimp, shelled and deveined, leaving tail part of shell on, if desired

2/3 cup fresh lemon juice (about 3 large lemons)
1/2 cup distilled white vinegar
1/2 cup vegetable oil
3 tablespoons pickling spices, tied in cheesecloth bag
2 teaspoons sugar
2 dill sprigs

1. In 4-quart saucepan combine *6 cups water*, sherry, 2 teaspoons salt, peppercorns, and bay leaf; heat to boiling over high heat. Add shrimp; heat to boiling. Shrimp should be opaque throughout when water returns to boil; if not, cook about 1 minute longer. Drain.
2. In large bowl, combine lemon juice, vinegar, oil, pickling spices, sugar, dill, and remaining 1 teaspoon salt. Add shrimp and toss well to coat. Spoon into zip-tight plastic bags, press out excess air, and seal. Refrigerate shrimp overnight to marinate, turning bags occasionally.
3. Remove shrimp from marinade and arrange in chilled bowl. Serve with cocktail picks.

Each serving: About 69 calories, 9g protein, 1g carbohydrate, 2g total fat (0g saturated), 0g fiber, 70mg cholesterol, 166mg sodium.

Vietnamese-Style Grilled Shrimp

Let each guest wrap a shrimp, rice vermicelli, green onions, and herbs in a lettuce leaf and dip the package into the Nuoc Cham.

PREP: 25 MINUTES PLUS STANDING   GRILL: 2 MINUTES
MAKES 12 APPETIZER SERVINGS

Nuoc Cham (below)
1 pound large shrimp, peeled and deveined
2 ounces rice stick noodles (rice vermicelli)
12 Boston lettuce leaves

12 cilantro sprigs
12 mint sprigs
12 basil sprigs
3 green onions, cut into 2" by 1/8" strips
1 lime, cut into wedges

1. Prepare Nuoc Cham. In medium bowl, marinate shrimp in 1/3 cup Nuoc Cham 15 minutes. Prepare rice stick noodles as label directs. Drain.
2. Arrange lettuce leaves on large platter. Arrange noodles, cilantro, mint, basil, and green onions on lettuce leaves. Scatter lime wedges around platter.
3. Prepare grill or preheat broiler. Grill shrimp over medium heat, or broil on rack in broiling pan, at closest position to heat source until opaque throughout, about 3 minutes per side.
4. To serve, place shrimp on lettuce leaves and serve with small bowls of remaining Nuoc Cham.

Each serving: About 55 calories, 9g protein, 2g carbohydrate, 1g total fat (0g saturated), 1g fiber, 58mg cholesterol, 467mg sodium.

Nuoc Cham

Combine 1/2 **cup water**, 6 **tablespoons Asian fish sauce (nam pla or nuoc nam)**, 1/4 **cup fresh lime juice**, 2 **tablespoons sugar**, 1 **garlic clove,** peeled and halved, and 1/8 **teaspoon ground red pepper (cayenne)** in a small bowl. Let stand at least 15 minutes; discard garlic. Makes 1 1/2 cups.

Shrimp Cocktail

Everyone loves to dip shrimp into sauce. So, here are two sauces that are very different but equally delicious.

PREP: 25 MINUTES PLUS CHILLING   COOK: 17 MINUTES
MAKES 8 FIRST-COURSE SERVINGS

1 lemon, thinly sliced
4 bay leaves
20 whole black peppercorns
10 whole allspice berries
2 teaspoons salt
24 extra-large shrimp (1 pound),
    shelled and deveined

Southwestern-Style Cocktail Sauce
   (page 177)
Mustard Dipping Sauce (page 177)
12 small romaine lettuce leaves
24 (7-inch) bamboo skewers

1. In 5-quart Dutch oven, combine *2 quarts water*, lemon, bay leaves, peppercorns, allspice berries, and salt; heat to boiling. Cover and boil 15 minutes.

2. Add shrimp and cook just until opaque throughout, 1 to 2 minutes. Drain; rinse shrimp with cold running water to stop cooking. Cover and refrigerate shrimp up to 24 hours.

3. Prepare Southwestern-Style Cocktail Sauce and/or Mustard Dipping Sauce.

4. Just before serving, place bowls of sauces in center of platter; arrange romaine leaves around bowls, leaf tips facing out. Thread each shrimp on a bamboo skewer and place skewers on romaine.

Each serving without sauce: About 51 calories, 10g protein, 1g carbohydrate, 1g total fat (0g saturated), 0g fiber, 70mg cholesterol, 141mg sodium.

Southwestern-Style Cocktail Sauce

In bowl, stir **1 cup bottled cocktail sauce, 2 tablespoons chopped fresh cilantro, 2 teaspoons minced jalapeño chile**, and **2 teaspoons fresh lime juice** until well combined. Cover and refrigerate up to 24 hours. Makes about 1 cup.

Each tablespoon: About 18 calories, 0g protein, 4g carbohydrate, 0g total fat (0g saturated), 0g fiber, 0mg cholesterol, 191mg sodium.

Mustard Dipping Sauce

In small serving bowl, stir **1 cup reduced-fat sour cream, 3 tablespoons grainy Dijon mustard, 3 tablespoons chopped fresh parsley, 1/4 teaspoon freshly grated lemon peel, 1/4 teaspoon salt**, and **1/8 teaspoon coarsely ground black pepper** until well combined. Cover and refrigerate up to 24 hours. Makes about 1 cup.

Each tablespoon: About 28 calories, 1g protein, 1g carbohydrate, 2g total fat (1g saturated), 1g fiber, 5mg cholesterol, 111mg sodium.

Clams Casino

These bacon and pepper studded clams have been an American favorite since they were created at the Casino restaurant in New York City in 1917.

PREP: 30 MINUTES BAKE: 10 MINUTES MAKES 6 FIRST-COURSE SERVINGS

2 dozen littleneck clams, scrubbed and shucked, bottom shells reserved
kosher or rock salt (optional)
3 slices bacon
1 tablespoon olive oil
1/2 red pepper, very finely chopped

1/2 green pepper, very finely chopped
1/4 teaspoon coarsely ground black pepper
1 garlic clove, finely chopped
1 cup fresh bread crumbs (about 2 slices bread)

1. Preheat oven to 425°F. Arrange clams in shells in jelly-roll pan lined with 1/2-inch layer of kosher salt to keep them flat, if desired; refrigerate.

2. In 10-inch skillet, cook bacon over medium heat until browned; transfer to paper towels to drain. Discard fat from skillet. Add oil, red and green peppers, and black pepper to skillet. Cook, stirring occasionally, until peppers are tender, about 5 minutes. Stir in garlic and cook 30 seconds; remove from heat.

3. Finely crumble bacon; stir bacon and bread crumbs into pepper mixture in skillet. Spoon crumb mixture evenly over clams. Bake until topping is lightly golden, about 10 minutes.

Each serving: About 107 calories, 9g protein, 6g carbohydrate, 5g total fat (1g saturated), 1g fiber, 23mg cholesterol, 122mg sodium.

Rumaki

These tasty appetizers can be marinated for one hour or up to overnight, then popped under the broiler at serving time.

PREP: 25 MINUTES PLUS MARINATING BROIL: 7 MINUTES
MAKES 16 RUMAKI

1/4 cup soy sauce
2 tablespoons brown sugar
2 tablespoons dry sherry
1/2 teaspoon ground ginger
8 thin slices bacon

1/4 cup drained sliced canned water
  chestnuts
12 ounces chicken livers, each cut in
  half and trimmed

1. In medium bowl, with wire whisk, mix soy sauce, brown sugar, sherry, and ginger.

2. Cut bacon slices crosswise in half; place 1 slice water chestnut in middle of each piece. Top each bacon piece with 1 chicken-liver half; wrap bacon around water chestnut and liver. Secure with toothpick.

3. Place rumaki in bowl with the soy mixture, tossing to coat. Cover and refrigerate at least 1 hour or up to overnight.

4. Preheat broiler. Place rumaki on rack in broiling pan. Broil 6 inches from heat source, turning once, until bacon is cooked and has browned, 7 to 8 minutes.

Each rumaki: About 107 calories, 9g protein, 3g carbohydrate, 6g total fat (2g saturated), 0g fiber, 88mg cholesterol, 639mg sodium.

Tortilla Spirals

Sensational-looking spirals are easy do-ahead party fare. There are two different fillings: smoked salmon and dried tomato. Both are delicious. For added color, use flavored tortillas like spinach or tomato.

PREP: 35 MINUTES PLUS CHILLING   MAKES ABOUT 144 APPETIZERS

SMOKED SALMON FILLING
- 1¹/₂ packages (8 ounces each) cream cheese, softened
- 4 ounces thinly sliced smoked salmon, chopped
- ¹/₄ cup loosely packed fresh dill, chopped
- 3 tablespoons capers, drained and chopped

DRIED TOMATO FILLING
- 1 package (8 ounces) cream cheese, softened
- 10 oil-packed dried tomatoes with herb seasoning, drained and chopped
- 1 container (5.2 ounces) spreadable cheese with pepper
- ¹/₃ cup loosely packed fresh basil leaves, chopped

8 (10-inch) flour tortillas

1. Prepare Smoked Salmon Filling: In medium bowl, combine cream cheese, smoked salmon, dill, and capers until blended.

2. Prepare Dried Tomato Filling: In medium bowl, combine cream cheese, dried tomatoes, spreadable cheese, and basil until blended.

3. Spread each filling evenly over 4 tortillas. Roll each tortilla up tightly, jelly-roll fashion. Wrap each roll in plastic wrap and refrigerate until firm enough to slice, at least 4 hours or up to overnight.

4. To serve, unwrap tortilla rolls and trim ends. Cut rolls into ¹/₂-inch-thick slices.

Each appetizer with salmon filling: About 28 calories, 1g protein, 2g carbohydrate, 2g total fat (1g saturated), 0g fiber, 6mg cholesterol, 76mg sodium.

Each appetizer with tomato filling: About 32 calories, 1g protein, 2g carbohydrate, 2g total fat (1g saturated), 0g fiber, 6mg cholesterol, 42mg sodium.

Tortilla Spirals

Panfried Steak and Onions on Grilled Bread

Green herb sauce is a natural with steak. And Afghan flatbread is a great alternative to Italian-style breads.

PREP: 40 MINUTES   COOK: 30 MINUTES   MAKES 12 APPETIZER SERVINGS

PANFRIED STEAK AND ONIONS
2 teaspoons olive oil
1 beef flank steak (1 1/2 pounds)
1/4 teaspoon coarsely ground black pepper
3/4 teaspoon salt
2 large red onions, thinly sliced

HERB SAUCE
1 cup loosely packed fresh parsley leaves, chopped
1 cup loosely packed fresh cilantro leaves, chopped

3 tablespoons olive oil
2 tablespoons red wine vinegar
1 small garlic clove, crushed with garlic press
1/4 teaspoon salt
1/4 teaspoon coarsely ground black pepper
pinch crushed red pepper

2 Italian-style grilled flatbreads (one 13 1/2-ounce package), warmed, or 1 Afghan flatbread (16 ounces), cut crosswise in half

1. Prepare Panfried Steak and Onions: In heavy 12-inch skillet (preferably cast iron), heat oil over high heat until very hot. Sprinkle flank steak with pepper and 1/2 teaspoon salt.

2. Add steak to hot skillet; reduce heat to medium–high. Cook 12 to 17 minutes for medium-rare (depending on thickness of meat) or until desired doneness, turning once. Transfer steak to cutting board.

3. Reduce heat to medium. Add onions and remaining 1/4 teaspoon salt and cook, stirring occasionally, until onions are tender and browned, 12 to 15 minutes.

4. Meanwhile, prepare Herb Sauce: In small bowl, combine parsley, cilantro, oil, vinegar, garlic, salt, black pepper, and crushed red pepper.

5. To serve, thinly slice flank steak. Drizzle 1 flatbread with 2 tablespoons Herb Sauce; top with sliced steak, sliced onion, 2 tablespoons Herb Sauce, and remaining flatbread. Cut sandwich into 12 pieces.

Each appetizer: About 245 calories, 14g protein, 23g carbohydrate, 10g total fat (3g saturated), 1g fiber, 29mg cholesterol, 318mg sodium.

Mushroom-Fontina Pita Melts

A great do-ahead appetizer: You can cook the mushroom mixture and shred the cheese up to three days in advance, then refrigerate separately until ready to use.

PREP: 50 MINUTES BAKE: 5 MINUTES MAKES 16 APPETIZER SERVINGS

3 tablespoons butter or margarine
1 sweet medium onion, finely
  chopped
1/4 teaspoon dried thyme
1 pound white mushrooms, trimmed
  and sliced
8 ounces shiitake mushrooms, stems
  removed and caps sliced

1/2 teaspoon salt
2 tablespoons brandy
8 mini (4-inch) pitas, cut horizontally
  in half and toasted
4 ounces Fontina cheese, shredded
  (1 cup)

1. In 12-inch skillet, melt 1 tablespoon butter over medium-high heat. Add onion and thyme, and cook until onion is golden, about 5 minutes. Stir in remaining 2 tablespoons butter until melted. Add white and shiitake mushrooms and salt; cook, stirring occasionally, until liquid has evaporated and mushrooms have browned, about 15 minutes. Add brandy to mushroom mixture; cook 1 minute, stirring. Transfer to bowl; cover and refrigerate up to 3 days. Let mushroom mixture stand 30 minutes at room temperature when ready to assemble pitas.

2. Preheat oven to 450°F. Arrange pitas, split side up, on 2 large cookie sheets. Top each pita half with 2 rounded tablespoons of mushroom mixture and sprinkle with 1 tablespoon Fontina. Bake pitas until heated through and cheese melts, 4 to 5 minutes. Cut each pita into 4 wedges.

Each serving: About 111 calories, 4g protein, 12g carbohydrate, 5g total fat (2g saturated), 1g fiber, 14mg cholesterol, 208mg sodium.

Mozzarella in Carrozza

Mozzarella in Carrozza

Mozzarella in carrozza, "mozzarella in a carriage," is usually deep-fried, but we prefer to panfry ours. It is served with a buttery anchovy sauce, which can be drizzled over each serving. Delicious!

PREP: 20 MINUTES   COOK: 5 MINUTES   MAKES 8 APPETIZER SERVINGS

8 ounces part-skim mozzarella
    cheese
8 slices firm white bread, crusts
    trimmed
2 large eggs, well beaten
1/4 cup milk
1/4 cup all-purpose flour
1/2 teaspoon salt

1/4 teaspoon ground black pepper
1/2 cup plain dried bread crumbs
3 tablespoons vegetable oil
4 tablespoons butter or margarine
8 anchovy fillets, drained
1 tablespoon chopped fresh parsley
1 teaspoon capers, drained
1 teaspoon fresh lemon juice

1. Stand mozzarella on its side and cut lengthwise into 4 equal slices. Place 1 slice cheese between 2 slices bread to form sandwich. Repeat with remaining cheese and bread.

2. Preheat oven to 200°F. In pie plate, with wire whisk, beat eggs and milk. On waxed paper, combine flour, salt, and pepper; spread bread crumbs on separate sheet of waxed paper. Dip sandwiches, one at a time, in flour mixture, shaking off excess, then in egg mixture, and finally in bread crumbs, shaking off excess.

3. In nonstick 12-inch skillet, heat oil over medium heat until hot. Add sandwiches; cook until golden brown, about 1 1/2 minutes per side. Cut each sandwich on diagonal in half. Arrange on platter in single layer. Keep warm in oven.

4. In same skillet, melt butter; add anchovies and cook, stirring constantly, 1 minute. Add parsley, capers, and lemon juice; cook 30 seconds longer. Transfer sauce to small bowl. Serve sauce with sandwiches.

Each serving: About 309 calories, 13g protein, 22g carbohydrate, 19g total fat (8g saturated), 0g fiber, 89mg cholesterol, 713mg sodium.

Grilled Pitas with Caramelized Onions and Goat Cheese

Long, slow cooking makes onions especially sweet. The onions can be cooked up to three days in advance—just bring them to room temperature before spooning over the goat-cheese topping. For a tasty change, try with whole-wheat pitas, crumbled feta cheese, and snipped dill.

PREP: 45 MINUTES   GRILL: 3 MINUTES   MAKES 8 APPETIZER SERVINGS

4 tablespoons olive oil
2 jumbo onions (1 pound each), coarsely chopped
1 teaspoon sugar
1/4 teaspoon salt
1/4 teaspoon dried tarragon

1/4 teaspoon dried thyme
4 (6-inch) pitas, cut horizontally in half
6 to 7 ounces mild goat cheese, crumbled
1 tablespoon chopped fresh parsley

1. In nonstick 12-inch skillet, heat 2 tablespoons oil over medium heat. Add onions, sugar, and salt. Cook, stirring frequently, until very soft, about 15 minutes. Reduce heat to medium-low and cook, stirring frequently, until onions are golden brown, about 20 minutes longer.

2. Prepare grill. In cup, combine remaining 2 tablespoons oil, tarragon, and thyme. Brush rough sides of pitas with herb mixture. Spread with goat cheese, then top with caramelized onions.

3. Place pitas, topping side up, on grill over low heat; grill until bottoms are crisp and topping is heated through, about 3 minutes.

4. To serve, sprinkle with parsley and cut each pita into 4 wedges.

Each serving: About 245 calories, 8g protein, 27g carbohydrate, 12g total fat (4g saturated), 2g fiber, 10mg cholesterol, 310mg sodium.

Grilled Pitas with Caramelized Onions and Goat Cheese

Nachos

As the story goes, in the 1940s, a group of Texas women were lunching at the Victory Club in Piedras Negras, Mexico (just across the border from Eagle Pass, Texas). Chef Ignacio "Nacho" Anaya was running low on his usual specials, so he quickly threw some ingredients together for a snack. He spread a little cheese on toasted tortillas, topped each with a jalapeño slice, and called them *Nacho's Especiales*.

PREP: 30 MINUTES BAKE: 5 MINUTES PER BATCH   MAKES 36 NACHOS

36 unbroken large tortilla chips
3 large ripe plum tomatoes, cut into
  1/4-inch pieces
1/3 cup chopped fresh cilantro
1/4 teaspoon salt
1 tablespoon vegetable oil
1 fully cooked chorizo sausage
  (3 ounces), finely chopped, or
  3/4 cup finely chopped pepperoni
  (3 ounces)

1 medium onion, finely chopped
1 garlic clove, finely chopped
1/2 teaspoon ground cumin
1 can (15 to 19 ounces) black beans,
  rinsed and drained
4 ounces Monterey Jack cheese,
  shredded (1 cup)
2 pickled jalapeño chiles, very thinly
  sliced

1. Preheat oven to 400°F. Arrange as many tortilla chips as will fit in single layer on two ungreased large cookie sheets. In small bowl, combine tomatoes, cilantro, and salt.

2. In 10-inch skillet, heat oil over medium heat. Add chorizo, onion, garlic, and cumin; cook, stirring, until onion is tender, about 5 minutes. Stir in beans, mashing with back of spoon; cover and cook until heated through.

3. Place 1 tablespoon mashed bean mixture on each tortilla chip. Sprinkle Jack cheese over beans and top each nacho with 1 slice jalapeño. Bake until cheese begins to melt, about 5 minutes.

4. Spoon about 1 teaspoon tomato mixture on each nacho. Transfer nachos to platter; keep warm. Repeat with remaining chips, bean mixture, cheese, and tomato mixture. Serve warm.

Each nacho: About 51 calories, 2g protein, 4g carbohydrate, 3g total fat (1g saturated), 1g fiber, 5mg cholesterol, 112mg sodium.

Quesadillas

PREP: 40 MINUTES   BAKE: 8 MINUTES   MAKES 48 APPETIZERS

1 tablespoon vegetable oil
1 large onion (12 ounces), finely
  chopped
1 green pepper, finely chopped
1 red pepper, finely chopped
1 garlic clove, finely chopped
1/4 teaspoon ground cumin
1/4 teaspoon salt

2 tablespoons chopped fresh cilantro
  plus leaves
12 (6- to 7-inch) flour tortillas
6 ounces Monterey Jack cheese with
  jalapeño chiles, shredded
  (11/2 cups)
1 hot red chile pepper (optional)

1. In nonstick 10-inch skillet, heat oil over medium heat. Add onion and green and red peppers; cook, stirring frequently, until tender, about 15 minutes. Add garlic, cumin, and salt; cook, stirring frequently, about 5 minutes longer. Remove from heat and stir in chopped cilantro.

2. Place 6 tortillas on surface. Spread pepper mixture on tortillas and sprinkle with Monterey Jack. Top with remaining tortillas to make 6 quesadillas. If not serving right away, cover and refrigerate up to 6 hours.

3. Preheat oven to 450°F. Place quesadillas on 2 large cookie sheets and bake until lightly browned, about 4 minutes per side. Cut each quesadilla into 8 wedges; top each wedge with a cilantro leaf. Garnish platter with chile pepper, if desired.

Each appetizer: About 50 calories, 2g protein, 6g carbohydrate, 2g total fat (1g saturated), 0g fiber, 4mg cholesterol, 75mg sodium.

Corn and Poblano Quesadillas

Roasted poblano chiles give these quesadillas a gentle—and delicious—kick, but you could substitute a roasted red or green pepper, or even canned green chiles, if you like.

PREP: 20 MINUTES PLUS STANDING   BROIL/COOK: 28 MINUTES
MAKES 32 APPETIZERS

2 poblano chiles or 1 red or green pepper
2 ears corn, husks and silk removed
2 teaspoons vegetable oil
4 green onions, thinly sliced
1/4 teaspoon ground cumin
1/4 teaspoon salt
1/4 teaspoon ground black pepper
2 tablespoons chopped fresh cilantro
8 (6- to 7-inch) flour tortillas
4 ounces Monterey Jack cheese, shredded (1 cup)

1. Preheat broiler. Line broiling pan with foil. Cut each poblano chile lengthwise in half; remove and discard stem and seeds. Arrange poblanos, cut side down, in prepared broiling pan. Place pan in broiler, 5 to 6 inches from heat source. Broil, without turning, until skin is charred and blistered, 8 to 10 minutes.

2. Wrap poblanos in foil and allow to steam at room temperature 15 minutes or until cool enough to handle. Remove from foil. Peel skin and discard. Seed poblanos; finely chop.

3. Meanwhile, cut corn kernels from cobs. In 10-inch skillet, heat oil over medium heat. Add corn, green onions, cumin, salt, and pepper; cook, stirring frequently, until corn is tender-crisp, 4 to 5 minutes. Remove from heat; stir in poblanos and cilantro.

4. Place 4 tortillas on surface. Spread corn mixture on tortillas; sprinkle with Monterey Jack. Top with remaining 4 tortillas to make 4 quesadillas.

5. Wipe skillet clean. Heat skillet over medium-high heat until hot. Add 1 quesadilla and cook until tortilla has browned lightly and cheese just begins to melt, 1 1/2 to 2 minutes per side. Cut into 8 wedges. Repeat with remaining quesadillas. Serve hot.

Each appetizer: About 49 calories, 3g protein, 8g carbohydrate, 2g total fat (1g saturated fat), 4g fiber, 4mg cholesterol, 100mg sodium.

Gravlax

This classic Scandinavian salt-and-dill-cured salmon is a great make-ahead dish for brunch or supper. Serve with thinly sliced cucumbers, Mustard Sauce, and pumpernickel bread.

PREP: 30 MINUTES PLUS 24 TO 36 HOURS TO MARINATE
MAKES ABOUT 16 FIRST-COURSE SERVINGS

2 pieces salmon fillet (1 pound each) with skin	2 tablespoons brandy or aquavit
3 tablespoons salt	1 bunch fresh dill
2 tablespoons sugar	lemon wedges
1 tablespoon cracked black pepper	Mustard Sauce (below)

1. With tweezers, remove any small bones from salmon fillets. In small bowl, combine salt, sugar, and pepper. Gently rub salt mixture on all sides of salmon; sprinkle with brandy.

2. Divide dill into 3 portions. Line bottom of medium baking dish with one-third of dill. Place 1 salmon fillet, skin side down, on dill; top with another one-third of dill. Place remaining fillet, skin side up, on dill; top with remaining dill.

3. Cover salmon with plastic wrap and set heavy plate (larger than salmon) on top; place two or three heavy cans on plate to weight down salmon. Refrigerate at least 24 hours but preferably 36 hours, turning over salmon and dill halfway through marinating.

4. Scrape dill and pepper from salmon and discard. Holding knife almost parallel to surface, cut salmon into very thin slices. Transfer to platter. Place lemon wedges around salmon and serve with Mustard Sauce.

Each serving with 1 tablespoon sauce: About 155 calories, 10g protein, 3g carbohydrate, 11g total fat (2g saturated), 0g fiber, 30mg cholesterol, 598mg sodium.

Mustard Sauce

In small bowl, whisk **1/2 cup Dijon mustard**, **1/2 cup vegetable oil**, **1/4 cup white wine vinegar**, **1/4 cup sugar**, and **1/8 teaspoon salt** until smooth. Stir in **1/4 cup chopped fresh dill**. Makes 1 1/2 cups.

Ribbon Sandwiches

Tea parties became a favorite way for American women to entertain their friends in the 1960s—and the fancier the food, the better! Thin ribbons of elegant "stacked" sandwiches were frequently found on tea trays. To make the most attractive sandwiches, choose breads of contrasting colors and fill the sandwiches with a variety of creamy fillings, such as cream cheese with minced nuts and pimiento-stuffed olives, chicken salad, finely chopped ham salad, and egg salad with minced sweet pickles.

PREP: 40 MINUTES   MAKES 24 RIBBON SANDWICHES

1 package (8 ounces) cream cheese, softened
2 small green onions, finely chopped
4 radishes, finely chopped
3 tablespoons chopped fresh parsley
1/8 teaspoon salt
1/8 teaspoon ground black pepper
18 very thin slices whole-wheat bread
12 very thin slices white bread

1. Line jelly-roll pan with damp paper towels.
2. In small bowl, combine cream cheese, green onions, radishes, parsley, salt, and pepper until well blended. For each stack, gently spread cream-cheese mixture on 2 slices whole-wheat bread and 2 slices white bread. Alternately stack slices, beginning with whole-wheat and ending with white. Place another slice whole-wheat bread on top of stack. Repeat with remaining bread to make 6 stacks.
3. Gently press down on each stack. With serrated knife, trim crusts. Place stacks in prepared pan; cover with additional damp paper towels to keep bread from drying out. Cover pan tightly with plastic wrap and refrigerate up to 4 hours.
4. Cut each stack crosswise into quarters. Arrange on a platter and serve.

Each sandwich: About 79 calories, 2g protein, 9g carbohydrate, 4g total fat (2g saturated), 3g fiber, 10mg cholesterol, 128mg sodium.

Smoked Salmon Tea Sandwiches

Using two different breads for these sandwiches is a nice touch.

PREP: 20 MINUTES   MAKES 32 TEA SANDWICHES

6 tablespoons butter or margarine,
  softened, or whipped cream cheese
8 very thin slices white bread

8 very thin slices whole-wheat bread
6 ounces very thinly sliced smoked
  salmon

1. Lightly spread butter on each bread slice. Arrange salmon on buttered side of white bread, trimming to fit. Top with whole-wheat bread. Trim crusts and cut each sandwich on diagonal into quarters.

2. If not serving immediately, line jelly-roll pan with damp paper towels. Place sandwiches in pan; cover with additional damp paper towels to keep bread from drying out. Cover pan tightly with plastic wrap and refrigerate up to 4 hours.

Each sandwich: About 43 calories, 2g protein, 3g carbohydrate, 3g total fat (1g saturated), 1g fiber, 7mg cholesterol, 166mg sodium.

Cucumber Tea Sandwiches

Utterly English and perfectly delicious, these classic sandwiches are a necessity at a tea party. A V-slicer or mandoline will make the thinnest cucumber slices.

PREP: 20 MINUTES PLUS CHILLING   MAKES 32 TEA SANDWICHES

1 English (seedless) cucumber
1/2 teaspoon salt
5 tablespoons butter or margarine, softened

16 very thin slices white or whole-wheat bread
32 fresh mint leaves (optional)

1. Cut cucumber lengthwise in half and crosswise into paper-thin slices. In colander set over bowl, toss together cucumber and salt. Cover and refrigerate 30 minutes, stirring occasionally. Discard liquid in bowl. Pat cucumber slices dry with paper towels.

2. Lightly spread butter on each bread slice. Arrange cucumber on 8 buttered slices; place 1 mint leaf, if using, in each corner of bread. Top with remaining bread slices. Trim crusts and cut each sandwich on diagonal into quarters.

3. If not serving right away, line jelly-roll pan with damp paper towels. Place sandwiches in pan; cover with additional damp paper towels to keep bread from drying out. Cover pan tightly with plastic wrap and refrigerate up to 4 hours.

Each sandwich: About 36 calories, 1g protein, 4g carbohydrate, 2g total fat (1g saturated), 1g fiber, 5mg cholesterol, 74mg sodium.

Watercress and Radish Tea Sandwiches

Spread butter on bread as in step 2 above. Lightly sprinkle with a pinch of salt and pepper. Arrange **tender leaves of watercress (from about half a bunch)** on half the slices; top with **very thin slices of radish (from about 3 radishes)**. Cover with remaining bread slices. Trim sandwiches; cut and store as above.

Each sandwich: About 39 calories, 1g protein, 4g carbohydrate, 2g total fat (1g saturated), 1g fiber, 6mg cholesterol, 71mg sodium.

Dilled-Egg Tea Sandwiches

Use this recipe for large-size sandwiches as well as delicate tea sandwiches. They're tasty either way.

PREP: 40 MINUTES   MAKES 18 TEA SANDWICHES

**3 large hard-cooked eggs, peeled and
  finely shredded**
1/4 cup mayonnaise
2 tablespoons chopped fresh dill
**1/4 teaspoon freshly grated lemon
  peel**

1/4 teaspoon ground black pepper
**12 very thin slices white or whole-
  wheat bread**

1. In medium bowl, combine eggs, mayonnaise, dill, lemon peel, and pepper. Spread evenly on 6 bread slices; top with remaining bread slices. Trim crusts and cut each sandwich into 3 equal rectangles.

2. If not serving right away, line jelly-roll pan with damp paper towels. Place sandwiches in pan; cover with additional damp paper towels to keep bread from drying out. Cover pan tightly with plastic wrap and refrigerate up to 4 hours.

*Each sandwich: About 68 calories, 2g protein, 6g carbohydrate, 4g total fat
(1g saturated), 1g fiber, 37mg cholesterol, 95mg sodium.*

Cheddar and Chutney Tea Sandwiches

This sweet-and-savory combination is a treat with a cup of tea or even a cocktail.

PREP: 15 MINUTES MAKES 16 TEA SANDWICHES

3 tablespoons butter or margarine, softened

3 tablespoons mango chutney, finely chopped

8 very thin slices white or whole-wheat bread

4 ounces Cheddar cheese, shredded (1 cup)

1. In small bowl, combine butter and chutney until well blended. Spread evenly on bread slices. Sprinkle Cheddar on buttered side of 4 bread slices. Top with remaining bread. Trim crusts and cut each sandwich into 4 squares or triangles.

2. If not serving right away, line jelly-roll pan with damp paper towels. Place sandwiches in pan; cover with additional damp paper towels to keep bread from drying out. Cover pan tightly with plastic wrap and refrigerate up to 4 hours.

Each sandwich: About 78 calories, 2g protein, 6g carbohydrate, 5g total fat (3g saturated), 1g fiber, 13mg cholesterol, 136mg sodium.

Cranberry-Fig Conserve with Brie

PREP: 10 MINUTES PLUS CHILLING   COOK: 15 MINUTES
MAKES 24 APPETIZER SERVINGS

2/3 cup packed brown sugar

2/3 cup water

1/4 cup brandy

1 lemon

1 bag (12 ounces) cranberries, picked over

8 ounces dried figs, stems trimmed and each cut into 8 pieces

1 jalapeño chile with seeds, chopped

1 wheel (6 to 7 inches in diameter) ripe Brie cheese or 1-pound wedge

1 loaf French bread, sliced (optional)

1. In 2-quart saucepan, combine brown sugar, water, and brandy. Heat to boiling over high heat; boil 2 minutes.

2. Meanwhile, from lemon, grate 1 teaspoon peel and squeeze 2 tablespoons juice. Add cranberries, figs, jalapeño, and lemon peel and juice to saucepan; heat to boiling, stirring frequently. Reduce heat to medium and cook, stirring occasionally, until most of cranberries pop and mixture thickens slightly, about 5 minutes.

3. Transfer cranberry mixture to bowl or container. Cover and refrigerate at least 3 hours or up to 1 week. Makes about 3 cups.

4. About 1 hour before serving, remove Brie and conserve from refrigerator; let stand at room temperature about 30 minutes to warm slightly. To serve, spoon some conserve over Brie if you like. Serve remaining conserve in small serving bowl along with sliced bread, if desired.

Each serving without bread: About 120 calories, 4g protein, 14g carbohydrate, 5g total fat (3g saturated), 2g fiber, 19mg cholesterol, 120mg sodium.

Savory Ricotta Cheesecake

This basil-scented cheesecake can be served warm or at room temperature with a salad of baby greens or tomatoes and crusty bread or cut into small squares for finger food.

PREP: 15 MINUTES BAKE: 1 HOUR 10 MINUTES
MAKES 12 FIRST-COURSE SERVINGS

2 garlic cloves, peeled
1 cup loosely packed fresh basil leaves
1 container (32 ounces) part-skim ricotta cheese
1 package (8 ounces) cream cheese
1/3 cup freshly grated Parmesan cheese

4 large eggs
3 tablespoons all-purpose flour
3/4 teaspoon freshly grated orange peel
1/2 teaspoon salt
1/4 teaspoon ground black pepper

1. Preheat oven to 350°F. Lightly grease 9-inch springform pan. Place on cookie sheet.

2. In 1-quart saucepan, heat *2 cups water* to boiling over high heat. Add garlic and cook 3 minutes to blanch. Drain.

3. In food processor with knife blade attached, process garlic and basil until chopped. Add ricotta, cream cheese, Parmesan, eggs, flour, orange peel, salt, and pepper; puree until smooth and well combined. Pour into prepared pan.

4. Bake until cake is just set and toothpick inserted in center comes out clean, about 1 hour 10 minutes. Cool in pan on wire rack for 10 minutes. With small knife, carefully loosen cheesecake from side of pan; remove side of pan. To serve, cut into wedges.

Each wedge: About 222 calories, 14g protein, 7g carbohydrate, 15g total fat (9g saturated), 0g fiber, 117mg cholesterol, 319mg sodium.

Fennel, Garlic, and Orange Barrel Olives

For the most flavor, be sure to buy the best olives you can. Try a specialty food store or the olive bar in your favorite supermarket.

PREP: 10 MINUTES PLUS MARINATING   MICROWAVE: 40 SECONDS
MAKES ABOUT 7 CUPS

2 tablespoons extravirgin olive oil
4 teaspoons fennel seeds, crushed
2 large garlic cloves, minced
2 pounds (about 4 pint containers)
   assorted unpitted olives, such as
   Kalamata, Italian oil cured, Niçoise,
   or large green, drained

1 teaspoon freshly grated orange
   peel
3 strips (3" by 1" each) orange peel

1. In microwave-safe cup, combine oil, fennel seeds, and garlic. Heat in microwave oven on High 40 to 60 seconds, or until just aromatic.
2. In large bowl, toss olives with hot oil mixture, orange peel, and orange-peel strips to coat. Cover bowl with plastic wrap and refrigerate, stirring occasionally, for at least 24 hours to allow flavors to develop. (Or, in large zip-tight plastic bag, combine all ingredients, turning olives to coat well. Seal bag, pressing out excess air. Place on plate; refrigerate, turning bag occasionally.) Store in refrigerator up to 1 month.

Each 1/4 cup: About 40 calories, 0g protein, 2g carbohydrate, 4g total fat (1g saturated), 1g fiber, 0mg cholesterol, 235mg sodium.

SAVORY SOUPS

Gazpacho

Chilled Cucumber Soup

Homemade curry oil adds a taste of the tropics to this summer favorite. A drizzle of bottled basil or lemon oil is also a delicious touch.

PREP: 25 MINUTES PLUS CHILLING   COOK: 3 MINUTES
MAKES ABOUT 4 CUPS OR 4 FIRST-COURSE SERVINGS

CUCUMBER SOUP
- 2 English (seedless) cucumbers (about 12 ounces each), peeled
- 1 small garlic clove, crushed with garlic press
- 1 container (16 ounces) plain low-fat yogurt
- 1/2 cup low-fat (1%) milk
- 1 tablespoon fresh lemon juice
- 1 1/4 teaspoons salt

CURRY OIL
- 2 tablespoons olive oil
- 1/2 teaspoon curry powder
- 1/2 teaspoon ground cumin
- 1/4 teaspoon crushed red pepper

- 1 small tomato, chopped
- 1 tablespoon thinly sliced fresh mint leaves

1. Prepare Cucumber Soup: Cut enough cucumber into 1/4-inch pieces to equal 1/2 cup; reserve for garnish. Cut remaining cucumber into chunks. In blender or in food processor with knife blade attached, combine cucumber chunks, garlic, yogurt, milk, lemon juice, and salt; blend until almost smooth. Pour mixture into medium bowl; cover and refrigerate at least 2 hours or until well chilled.

2. Meanwhile, prepare Curry Oil: In small saucepan, combine oil, curry powder, cumin, and crushed red pepper. Cook over low heat until mixture is fragrant and oil is hot, about 3 minutes. Remove from heat; strain curry oil through fine mesh sieve into cup.

3. In small bowl, combine tomato and reserved cucumber. To serve, stir soup and ladle into bowls. Spoon cucumber mixture into center of each bowl of soup. Sprinkle with mint and drizzle with Curry Oil.

Each serving: About 170 calories, 8g protein, 15g carbohydrate, 9g total fat (2g saturated), 2g fiber, 8mg cholesterol, 830mg sodium.

Chilled Cucumber Soup

Vichyssoise

This luxurious soup, traditionally served cold, is just as delicious hot (just call it cream of potato and leek soup). Either way, serve in small cups and garnish with freshly chopped chives.

PREP: 20 MINUTES PLUS CHILLING   COOK: 55 MINUTES
MAKES ABOUT 8 CUPS OR 8 FIRST-COURSE SERVINGS

4 medium leeks (1 1/4 pounds)
2 tablespoons butter or margarine
1 pound all-purpose potatoes
   (3 medium), peeled and thinly
   sliced
2 cans (14 to 14 1/2 ounces each)
   chicken broth

1/2 cup water
1 teaspoon salt
1/4 teaspoon ground black pepper
1 cup milk
1/2 cup heavy or whipping cream

1. Cut off roots and trim dark green tops from leeks; cut each leek lengthwise in half. Cut enough of white and pale green parts crosswise into 1/4-inch pieces to equal 4 1/2 cups. (Reserve any leftover leeks for another use.) Rinse leeks in large bowl of cold water, swishing to remove sand; transfer to colander to drain, leaving sand in bottom of bowl.

2. In 4-quart saucepan, melt butter over medium heat; add leeks and cook, stirring occasionally, 8 to 10 minutes. Add potatoes, broth, water, salt, and pepper; heat to boiling over high heat. Reduce heat; cover and simmer 30 minutes.

3. Spoon half of mixture into blender. Cover, with center part of cover removed to let steam escape; puree until smooth. Pour puree into bowl. Repeat with remaining potato mixture.

4. Stir milk and cream into puree. To serve hot, return soup to same clean saucepan and heat through over low heat (do not boil). To serve cold, cover and refrigerate at least 4 hours or until well chilled.

Each serving: About 161 calories, 4g protein, 14g carbohydrate, 10g total fat (6g saturated), 2g fiber, 32mg cholesterol, 778mg sodium.

Spicy Curried Carrot Soup

For spice without too much heat, use a good-quality mild Madras-style curry powder. Briefly sautéing the curry powder releases all its complex flavors.

PREP: 25 MINUTES   COOK: 45 MINUTES

MAKES ABOUT 13 CUPS OR 12 FIRST-COURSE SERVINGS

2 tablespoons olive oil
1 jumbo onion (1 pound), chopped
4 teaspoons curry powder
1 tablespoon grated, peeled fresh
  ginger
3 bags (16 ounces each) carrots,
  peeled and coarsely chopped

2 cans (14 to 14 1/2 ounces each)
  chicken broth
6 cups water
1 1/2 teaspoons salt
1 cup half-and-half or light cream

1. In 5-quart Dutch oven, heat oil over medium heat. Add onion; cook until tender and golden, 10 to 15 minutes.

2. Add curry powder and ginger; cook, stirring constantly, 1 minute. Add carrots, broth, 2 cups water, and salt; heat to boiling. Reduce heat; cover and simmer until carrots are very tender, about 20 minutes. Cool slightly.

3. Spoon one-fourth of carrot mixture into blender. Cover, with center part of cover removed to let steam escape; puree until smooth. Pour puree into bowl. Repeat with remaining carrot mixture.

4. Return puree to same clean Dutch oven; stir in half-and-half and remaining 4 cups water. Heat through over medium heat, stirring frequently (do not boil).

Each serving: About 115 calories, 3g protein, 15g carbohydrate, 5g total fat (2g saturated), 4g fiber, 7mg cholesterol, 621mg sodium.

Gazpacho

Gazpacho

This delicious and refreshing chilled soup originated in Spain. Make it in summer when ripe red tomatoes and other favorite vegetables from the garden are at their peak.

PREP: 30 MINUTES PLUS CHILLING
MAKES ABOUT 6 1/2 CUPS OR 6 FIRST-COURSE SERVINGS

- 2 medium cucumbers (about 8 ounces each), peeled and seeded
- 2 pounds ripe tomatoes (about 6 medium), seeded and chopped
- 1/2 medium red pepper, coarsely chopped
- 1 garlic clove, chopped
- 1/2 cup water
- 3 tablespoons fresh lemon juice
- 1 tablespoon olive oil
- 1 teaspoon salt
- 1/8 teaspoon coarsely ground black pepper
- 1 cup fresh corn kernels (from 2 ears)
- 1 ripe avocado, pitted and cut into 1/2-inch pieces
- 1/4 cup thinly sliced red onion

1. Cut 1 cucumber into 1/4-inch pieces; cut remaining cucumber into chunks.

2. In large bowl, combine cucumber chunks, tomatoes, red pepper, garlic, water, lemon juice, oil, salt, and black pepper. Spoon half of mixture into blender; puree until smooth. Pour into bowl. Repeat with remaining tomato mixture.

3. Pour tomato mixture into large bowl; stir in chopped cucumber. Cover and refrigerate until well chilled, about 3 hours or up to overnight.

4. To serve, ladle soup into bowls and top with corn, avocado, and onion.

Each serving: About 145 calories, 3g protein, 19g carbohydrate, 8g total fat (1g saturated), 5g fiber, 0mg cholesterol, 470mg sodium.

Creamy Asparagus Soup

A classic soup to welcome the spring season! Serve with crispy breadsticks.

PREP: 10 MINUTES   COOK: 25 MINUTES
MAKES 5 1/2 CUPS OR 4 FIRST-COURSE SERVINGS

1 tablespoon butter or margarine
1 small onion, coarsely chopped
1 1/2 pounds asparagus, trimmed and coarsely chopped
1 can (14 to 14 1/2 ounces) chicken broth or vegetable broth
1 cup water

1/2 teaspoon salt
1/8 teaspoon ground black pepper
1/4 cup heavy or whipping cream
sliced green onions (optional)
steamed thin asparagus spears (optional)

1. In 4-quart saucepan, melt butter over medium heat. Add onion and cook, stirring frequently, until tender and lightly golden, 8 to 10 minutes. Add asparagus and cook, stirring occasionally, 5 minutes.

2. Add broth, water, salt, and pepper; heat to boiling over high heat. Reduce heat to low; cover and simmer until asparagus is very tender, 8 to 10 minutes. Remove from heat.

3. In blender, with center part of cover removed to allow steam to escape, puree asparagus mixture, in small batches, until smooth. Pour each batch puree into bowl. (If you like, use hand blender to puree mixture in saucepan.).

4. Return soup to saucepan. Stir in cream and heat through. Ladle soup into bowls; top with green onions and asparagus spears, if you like.

Each serving: About 126 calories, 4g protein, 5g carbohydrate, 10g total fat (6g saturated), 2g fiber, 29mg cholesterol, 794mg sodium.

Creamy Asparagus Soup

Cream of Mushroom Soup

This mushroom-laden soup is very versatile. Use one variety or a mix of favorites to alter the soup's flavor. Some flavorful possibilities are creminis, shiitakes, and portobellos.

PREP: 20 MINUTES   COOK: 35 MINUTES

MAKES ABOUT 6 CUPS OR 6 FIRST-COURSE SERVINGS

3 tablespoons butter or margarine
1 pound mushrooms, trimmed and thinly sliced
1 medium onion, thinly sliced
2 tablespoons all-purpose flour
2 cups water
1 can (14 to 14 1/2 ounces) chicken broth
1/2 teaspoon fresh thyme or 1/4 teaspoon dried thyme
1/2 teaspoon salt
1/8 teaspoon ground black pepper
1/2 cup heavy or whipping cream

1. In 5-quart Dutch oven, melt 2 tablespoons butter over medium-high heat. Add mushrooms and cook, stirring occasionally, until mushrooms are tender and begin to brown, about 15 minutes. Transfer to bowl.

2. In same Dutch oven, melt remaining 1 tablespoon butter over medium heat. Add onion and cook until tender and golden, about 10 minutes.

3. Stir in flour until blended; cook 1 minute. Gradually stir in water, broth, thyme, salt, pepper, and half of mushrooms; heat to boiling, stirring constantly.

4. Spoon half of mushroom mixture into blender. Cover, with center part of cover removed to let steam escape; puree until smooth. Pour puree into bowl. Repeat with remaining mixture.

5. Return puree to same clean Dutch oven; stir in cream and remaining mushrooms with their juice. Heat through (do not boil).

Each serving: About 167 calories, 3g protein, 9g carbohydrate, 14g total fat (8g saturated), 1g fiber, 43mg cholesterol, 548mg sodium.

Potato and Chive Soup

A delicious creamy soup made with yellow potatoes, vegetables, and chicken broth . . . but not a drop of cream.

PREP: 15 MINUTES   COOK: 30 MINUTES
MAKES ABOUT 6 CUPS OR 6 FIRST-COURSE SERVINGS

2 tablespoons butter or margarine
1 medium onion, chopped
1 medium stalk celery, chopped
1 carrot, peeled and chopped
2 garlic cloves, minced
1 1/4 pounds yellow potatoes, such
 as Yukon Gold, peeled and cut into
 1/2-inch pieces

3 cups water
1 can (14 to 14 1/2 ounces) chicken
 broth
3/4 teaspoon salt
1/4 teaspoon coarsely ground black
 pepper
1/4 cup snipped fresh chives

1. In 4-quart saucepan, melt butter over medium heat. Add onion, celery, and carrot; cook, stirring occasionally, until vegetables are tender, about 10 minutes. Add garlic; cook, stirring 1 minute. Add potatoes, water, broth, salt, and pepper; heat to boiling over high heat. Reduce heat to low; simmer, uncovered, until potatoes are tender, about 15 minutes.

2. In blender, with center part of cover removed to allow steam to escape, puree potato mixture, in small batches, until smooth. Pour each batch puree into bowl. (If you like, use hand blender to puree mixture in saucepan.)

3. Return soup to saucepan; heat through over medium heat, stirring occasionally. Remove from heat; stir in chives.

Each serving: About 163 calories, 4g protein, 26g carbohydrate, 4g total fat (2g saturated), 3g fiber, 10mg cholesterol, 145mg sodium.

Roasted Butternut Squash and Apple Bisque

PREP: 30 MINUTES BAKE/COOK: 1 HOUR 15 MINUTES
MAKES ABOUT 12 CUPS OR 12 FIRST-COURSE SERVINGS

1¹/₂ pounds Granny Smith apples,
  peeled, cored, and quartered
4¹/₂ pounds butternut squash (about
  3 medium), each cut lengthwise in
  half and seeded
1 large onion (about 12 ounces),
  peeled and cut into quarters
3 tablespoons olive oil
¹/₄ cup packed brown sugar
³/₄ teaspoon ground cinnamon

¹/₂ teaspoon ground cardamom
¹/₂ teaspoon salt
¹/₂ teaspoon ground black pepper
  plus coarsely ground pepper
3 cans (14 to 14¹/₂ ounces each)
  chicken broth
2 cups water
plain low-fat yogurt (optional)
fresh chives

1. Preheat oven to 425°F. Divide apples, squash (cut side up), and onion between two 15¹/₂" by 10¹/₂" jelly-roll pans or shallow large roasting pans. Drizzle with oil; toss onions and apples to coat with oil. In cup, combine brown sugar, cinnamon, cardamom, salt, and pepper. Sprinkle spice mixture over squash mixture in pans. Roast until very tender and golden, about 1 hour, rotating pans between upper and lower racks halfway through roasting time. Cool slightly.

2. With spoon, scoop flesh from squash halves and place in medium bowl. Discard any dark, tough bottom layers from onion quarters. Cut onion and apples into large chunks.

3. Spoon one-third of roasted vegetable mixture along with 1 can broth into blender. Cover, with center part of cover removed to let steam escape; puree until smooth. Pour puree into 4-quart saucepan. Repeat with remaining vegetable mixture and broth. Add water to pureed soup mixture; heat to boiling over high heat. Reduce heat to low; cover and simmer 5 minutes. (If not serving soup right away, spoon into large bowl; cover and refrigerate up to 2 days. Or ladle soup into

freezer-safe containers and freeze up to 1 month. Thaw in refrigerator overnight; to serve, reheat over medium heat.)

4. To serve, ladle soup into soup bowls and swirl some yogurt into each, if you like. Garnish with chives and sprinkle with coarsely ground pepper.

Each serving: About 140 calories, 2g protein, 26g carbohydrate, 5g total fat (1g saturated), 5g fiber, 0mg cholesterol, 540mg sodium.

Roasted Butternut Squash and Apple Bisque

Porcupine Meatballs

Porcupine Meatballs

When these meatballs are poached in fragrant chicken broth, the rice cooks and expands, so the meatballs end up resembling porcupines.

PREP: 30 MINUTES   COOK: 40 MINUTES
MAKES 8 FIRST-COURSE SERVINGS

1 tablespoon vegetable oil
1/2 small red pepper, finely chopped (1/2 cup) plus additional 2" by 1/4" matchstick strips
3 green onions, finely chopped plus additional green onions cut into 2" by 1/4" matchstick strips
2 garlic cloves, crushed with garlic press
1 tablespoon minced, peeled fresh ginger plus four 1/4-inch-thick slices

1 pound ground pork
1/2 cup long-grain white rice
1 large egg
1 tablespoon soy sauce
1/8 teaspoon ground red pepper (cayenne)
1 1/2 cups water
1 can (14 to 14 1/2 ounces) chicken broth
1/4 teaspoon Asian sesame oil

1. In deep 10-inch skillet, heat vegetable oil over medium-high heat until hot. Add finely chopped red pepper; cook, stirring occasionally, just until tender, about 5 minutes. Add finely chopped green onions, garlic, and minced ginger; cook, stirring, 1 minute.

2. Transfer vegetable mixture to medium bowl. Stir in ground pork, uncooked rice, egg, soy sauce, and ground red pepper until well blended but not overmixed.

3. Line 15 1/2" by 10 1/2" jelly-roll pan with waxed paper. With damp hands, shape meat mixture by rounded tablespoons into thirty-two 1 1/2-inch meatballs (mixture will be soft); place in jelly-roll pan.

4. In same skillet (no need to wash it), combine water, broth, sesame oil, and sliced ginger; heat to boiling over high heat. Carefully lower meatballs into simmering broth (skillet will be very full); heat to boiling. Reduce heat to low; cover and simmer 30 minutes.

5. To serve, ladle meatballs and broth into large shallow bowls and sprinkle with green onion and red pepper strips.

Each serving: About 238 calories, 13g protein, 11g carbohydrate, 16g total fat (5g saturated), 0g fiber, 63mg cholesterol, 340mg sodium.

Shrimp Bisque

Typically, a bisque is a thick, rich, creamy soup made by pureeing stock that contains cooked seafood or sometimes vegetables. Ours gets an extra flavor boost by simmering the shrimp shells in stock. Lacing the soup with cream and brandy just before serving makes it even more delicious.

PREP: 20 MINUTES COOK: 1 HOUR 20 MINUTES

MAKES ABOUT 10 CUPS OR 10 FIRST-COURSE SERVINGS

3 tablespoons butter or margarine	2 tablespoons regular long-grain rice
1 pound medium shrimp, shelled and deveined, shells reserved	1 bay leaf
	1 1/4 teaspoons salt
2 cans (14 1/2 ounces each) low-sodium chicken broth	1/8 to 1/4 teaspoon ground red pepper (cayenne)
1 cup dry white wine	1 can (14 to 14 1/2 ounces) diced tomatoes
1/2 cup water	
1 large onion (12 ounces), chopped	1 cup half-and-half or light cream
2 carrots, peeled and chopped	2 tablespoons brandy or dry sherry
2 stalks celery, chopped	

1. In nonreactive 5-quart Dutch oven, melt 1 tablespoon butter over medium heat. Add shrimp shells and cook, stirring frequently, 5 minutes. Add broth, wine, and water; heat to boiling. Reduce heat; cover and simmer 15 minutes. Strain broth mixture through sieve into bowl; with spoon, press on shrimp shells to extract any remaining liquid. Discard shells.

2. In same clean Dutch oven, melt remaining 2 tablespoons butter over medium-high heat. Add shrimp and cook until opaque throughout, about 3 minutes. With slotted spoon, transfer shrimp to separate bowl. Add onion, carrots, and celery to Dutch oven; cook, stirring, until celery is tender, about 10 minutes. Add shrimp broth, rice, bay leaf, salt, and ground red pepper; heat to boiling over high heat. Reduce heat; cover and simmer until rice is tender, about 20 minutes. Add tomatoes with their juice and cook 10 minutes longer. Remove from heat and discard bay leaf. Stir in shrimp.

3. Spoon one-fourth of shrimp mixture into blender. Cover, with center part of cover removed to let steam escape; puree until very smooth. Pour puree into bowl. Repeat with remaining mixture.

4. Return puree to same clean Dutch oven; stir in half-and-half and brandy. Heat through over medium heat (do not boil).

Each serving: About 149 calories, 10g protein, 9g carbohydrate, 7g total fat (4g saturated), 1g fiber, 74mg cholesterol, 667mg sodium.

Sorrel Soup

Delicate, lemony-tart sorrel is always a sign of spring. When cooked, it tints this soup a lovely pale green.

PREP: 20 MINUTES   COOK: 25 MINUTES
MAKES ABOUT 4 2/3 CUPS OR 4 FIRST-COURSE SERVINGS

8 ounces fresh sorrel, stems removed
1 tablespoon butter or margarine
1 medium onion, chopped
3 tablespoons all-purpose flour
1 can (14 to 14 1/2 ounces) chicken broth

2 cups water
1/8 teaspoon salt
pinch ground black pepper
1/2 cup heavy or whipping cream

1. Roll up several sorrel leaves together, cigar fashion, and thinly slice (about 4 1/4 cups). Reserve 1/4 cup sliced leaves.

2. In 3-quart saucepan, melt butter over medium heat. Add onion and cook, stirring frequently, until tender, about 8 minutes. Stir in 4 cups sliced sorrel and cook, stirring frequently, until completely wilted. Add flour and cook, stirring, 1 minute.

3. Gradually stir in broth, water, salt, and pepper. Heat to boiling over high heat. Reduce heat and simmer 5 minutes.

4. Spoon one-fourth of sorrel mixture into blender. Cover, with center part of cover removed to let steam escape; puree until smooth. Pour puree into bowl. Repeat with remaining mixture.

5. Return puree to same clean saucepan; stir in cream and heat through (do not boil). Ladle soup into soup bowls and sprinkle with reserved sliced sorrel.

Each serving: About 187 calories, 3g protein, 11g carbohydrate, 15g total fat (9g saturated), 1g fiber, 49mg cholesterol, 545mg sodium.

Calico Cheese Soup

PREP: 15 MINUTES COOK: 15 MINUTES
MAKES ABOUT 6 CUPS OR 6 FIRST-COURSE SERVINGS

4 tablespoons butter or margarine
1 small garlic clove, crushed with garlic press
2 cups (1/2-inch) fresh bread pieces (about 6 slices crustless firm white bread)
1 large onion (12 ounces), chopped
2 carrots, peeled and chopped
1/2 cup chopped celery

1/4 cup all-purpose flour
1/4 teaspoon ground red pepper (cayenne)
3 cups canned chicken broth
1 cup half-and-half or light cream
8 ounces sharp Cheddar cheese, shredded (2 cups)

1. Preheat oven to 350°F. Melt 1 tablespoon butter. In medium bowl, combine melted butter and garlic. Add bread pieces, tossing to coat. Spread bread pieces in single layer in small baking pan. Bake, stirring once, until golden, about 15 minutes; set aside to cool.

2. In large saucepan, melt remaining 3 tablespoons butter over medium heat. Add onion, carrots, and celery. Cover and cook, stirring occasionally, until tender but not browned, about 10 minutes.

3. With wire whisk, stir in flour and ground red pepper until blended; cook, stirring, 2 minutes. Gradually whisk in broth and half-and-half until smooth; heat to boiling. Reduce heat to low. Stir in Cheddar; heat until melted (do not boil). Serve with croutons.

Each serving with croutons: About 384 calories, 15g protein, 22g carbohydrate, 26g total fat (16g saturated), 2g fiber, 77mg cholesterol, 511mg sodium.

Black Bean Soup

For thousands of years, black beans have been popular throughout Mexico and Venezuela. But it wasn't until 1970 that this soup began appearing on American menus. At that time, the Coach House restaurant in New York began serving a pureed black bean soup that contained a splash of sherry and was topped with a slice of lemon and some chopped hard-cooked egg.

PREP: 20 MINUTES PLUS OVERNIGHT TO SOAK BEANS
COOK: 2 HOURS 30 MINUTES
MAKES ABOUT 13 CUPS OR 12 FIRST-COURSE SERVINGS

1 pound dry black beans	2 smoked ham hocks (1 1/2 pounds)
3 tablespoons olive oil	10 cups water
3 large carrots, peeled and chopped	1 teaspoon coarsely ground black pepper
3 medium onions, chopped	
3 stalks celery with leaves, chopped	1/2 cup chopped fresh parsley
4 garlic cloves, peeled	3 tablespoons dry sherry
2 bay leaves	2 teaspoons salt
1/2 teaspoon dried thyme	12 paper-thin lemon slices

1. In large bowl, place beans with enough *water* to cover by 2 inches. Soak overnight.

2. Drain and rinse beans. In 5-quart Dutch oven, heat oil over medium heat. Add carrots, onions, and celery; cook, stirring, until tender, about 10 minutes. Add garlic, bay leaves, and thyme; cook 1 minute.

3. Add beans, ham hocks, water, and pepper to Dutch oven; heat to boiling over high heat. Reduce heat; cover and simmer until beans are very tender, about 2 hours. Discard ham hocks and bay leaves.

4. Spoon one-fourth of bean mixture into blender. Cover, with center part of cover removed to let steam escape; puree until very smooth. Pour into bowl. Repeat with remaining mixture. Return puree to same clean Dutch oven; stir in all but 2 tablespoons parsley, sherry, and salt. Cook 5 minutes.

5. To serve, ladle soup into bowls, garnish with lemon slices, and sprinkle with remaining 2 tablespoons parsley.

Each serving: About 207 calories, 10g protein, 32g carbohydrate, 5g total fat (1g saturated), 3g fiber, 2mg cholesterol, 788mg sodium.

Fresh Tomato Soup

Bring back those fond childhood memories with a hearty pot of cream of tomato soup. This one's a fresh take on the old-fashioned favorite. It starts with four pounds of garden-ripe tomatoes. (When fresh tomatoes are not at their best, substitute three 28-ounce cans.) To turn it into the creamy version we've all come to love, stir in some heavy cream just before serving.

PREP: 20 MINUTES   COOK: 1 HOUR 10 MINUTES
MAKES ABOUT 8 CUPS OR 8 FIRST-COURSE SERVINGS

1 tablespoon butter or margarine	1 can (14 to 14 1/2 ounces)
1 medium onion, chopped	chicken broth
1 stalk celery, chopped	1/2 cup water
1 carrot, peeled and chopped	1 bay leaf
1 garlic clove, crushed with garlic	3/4 teaspoon salt
press	1/4 teaspoon coarsely ground black
2 teaspoons fresh thyme or	pepper
1/2 teaspoon dried thyme	snipped fresh chives
4 pounds ripe tomatoes, coarsely	
chopped	

1. In nonreactive 5-quart Dutch oven, melt butter over low heat. Add onion, celery, and carrot; cook, stirring occasionally, until tender, about 10 minutes. Stir in garlic and thyme; cook 1 minute.

2. Add tomatoes, broth, water, bay leaf, salt, and pepper to Dutch oven; heat to boiling over high heat. Reduce heat; simmer until tomatoes are broken up and mixture has thickened slightly, about 45 minutes. Discard bay leaf.

3. Spoon one-third of mixture into blender. Cover, with center part of cover removed to let steam escape; puree until smooth. Pour puree into large bowl. Repeat with remaining mixture.

4. To serve hot, return soup to same clean Dutch oven and heat through. Ladle soup into bowls and sprinkle with chives. To serve cold, refrigerate at least 6 hours, or until well chilled.

Each serving: About 81 calories, 3g protein, 14g carbohydrate, 3g total fat (1g saturated), 3g fiber, 4mg cholesterol, 475mg sodium.

SWEET FINALES

Appel Strudel

Apple Strudel

Layer upon layer of delicate phyllo surround a tender apple filling. Try one of the variations too.

PREP: 1 HOUR PLUS COOLING   BAKE: 35 MINUTES   MAKES 10 SERVINGS

8 tablespoons butter or margarine (1 stick)	1/4 cup walnuts, toasted and ground
4 pounds Granny Smith apples (8 large), peeled, cored, and cut into 1/2-inch pieces	1/4 cup plain dried bread crumbs
	1/2 teaspoon ground cinnamon
	1/4 teaspoon ground nutmeg
1/2 cup dark seedless raisins	8 sheets (16" by 12" each) fresh or frozen (thawed) phyllo
2/3 plus 1/4 cup granulated sugar	confectioners' sugar

1. Prepare filling: In 12-inch skillet, melt 2 tablespoons butter over medium heat. Add apples, raisins, and 2/3 cup granulated sugar. Cook, stirring occasionally, 15 minutes. Increase heat to medium-high; cook until liquid has evaporated and apples are soft and golden, about 15 minutes longer. Remove from heat; cool filling completely.

2. Meanwhile, in small bowl, combine walnuts, bread crumbs, remaining 1/4 cup granulated sugar, cinnamon, and nutmeg.

3. Preheat oven to 400°F. In 1-quart saucepan, melt remaining 6 tablespoons butter. Cut two 24-inch lengths of waxed paper. Overlap two long sides by about 2 inches.

4. On waxed paper, place 1 phyllo sheet; lightly brush with some melted butter. Sprinkle with scant 2 tablespoons bread-crumb mixture. Repeat layering with remaining phyllo, melted butter, and crumb mixture; reserve about 1 tablespoon melted butter.

5. Spoon cooled apple filling along a long side of phyllo, covering about one-third of phyllo, and leaving 3/4-inch borders. Starting from filling side, roll phyllo up, jelly-roll fashion, using waxed paper to help lift roll. Place roll, seam side down, on diagonal, on ungreased large cookie sheet. Tuck ends of roll under; brush with reserved 1 tablespoon melted butter. Place two foil sheets under cookie sheet; crimp edges to form rim to catch any overflow during baking.

6. Bake strudel until phyllo is golden and filling is heated through, 35 to 40 minutes. If necessary, cover strudel loosely with foil during last 10 minutes of baking to prevent overbrowning. Cool on cookie sheet on wire rack about 20 minutes. To serve, dust with confectioners' sugar and cut into thick slices.

Each serving: About 338 calories, 2g protein, 58g carbohydrate, 13g total fat (6g saturated), 4g fiber, 25mg cholesterol, 192mg sodium.

Cheese Strudel

In large bowl, with mixer at medium speed, beat **1 package (8 ounces) cream cheese**, softened, **1/4 cup sugar**, and **1 tablespoon cornstarch** until thoroughly blended. With rubber spatula, fold in **1 cup ricotta cheese**, **1 teaspoon freshly grated lemon peel**, and **1/2 teaspoon vanilla extract** until well combined. Cover and refrigerate filling while preparing phyllo. Prepare and fill strudel as directed but substitute cheese filling for apple filling. Bake as directed.

Each serving: About 301 calories, 6g protein, 23g carbohydrate, 21g total fat (12g saturated), 1g fiber, 56mg cholesterol, 255mg sodium.

Dried Fruit Strudel

In 2-quart saucepan, combine **2 cups mixed dried fruit**, cut into 1-inch pieces, **1 cup dried figs**, cut into 1-inch pieces, **2 strips (3" by 1" each) lemon peel**, **1 cinnamon stick (3 inches)**, and **1 3/4 cups water**; heat to boiling over high heat, stirring occasionally. Reduce heat to medium; cook until all liquid has been absorbed and fruit is tender, about 20 minutes longer. Cool completely. Prepare and fill strudel as directed but substitute dried fruit filling for apple filling. Bake as directed.

Each serving: About 285 calories, 3g protein, 49g carbohydrate, 10g total fat (5g saturated), 6g fiber, 19mg cholesterol, 175mg sodium.

Cherry Strudel

In 4-quart saucepan, combine **2 cans (16 ounces each) tart (sour) cherries packed in water**, drained (¹/₂ cup liquid reserved), **1 cup sugar**, **¹/₄ cup cornstarch**, **1 tablespoon fresh lemon juice**, and **¹/₄ teaspoon ground cinnamon**; heat to boiling over medium-high heat, stirring constantly. Reduce heat to medium-low; boil 1 minute. Remove from heat; stir in ¹/₂ **teaspoon vanilla extract**. Cool completely. Prepare and fill strudel as directed but substitute cherry filling for apple filling. Bake as directed.

Each serving: About 280 calories, 3g protein, 47g carbohydrate, 10g total fat (5g saturated), 2g fiber, 19mg cholesterol, 174mg sodium.

Chocolate Fondue with Fruit

PREP: 15 MINUTES   COOK: 5 MINUTES   MAKES 8 SERVINGS

6 squares (6 ounces) semisweet
chocolate, coarsely chopped

1/2 cup half-and-half or light cream

1/2 teaspoon vanilla extract

4 small bananas, peeled and cut into
1/2-inch-thick slices

2 to 3 small pears, cored and cut into
1/2-inch-thick wedges

1 pint strawberries, hulled

1/2 cup finely chopped almonds,
toasted

1. In heavy 1-quart saucepan, heat chocolate and half-and-half over low heat, stirring frequently, until chocolate has melted and mixture is smooth, about 5 minutes. Stir in vanilla; keep warm.

2. To serve, arrange bananas, pears, and strawberries on large platter. Spoon sauce into small bowl; place nuts in separate small bowl. With forks or toothpicks, have guests dip fruit into chocolate sauce, then into nuts.

Each serving: About 249 calories, 4g protein, 36g carbohydrate, 13g total fat (5g saturated), 1g fiber, 6mg cholesterol, 10mg sodium.

Holiday Citrus Platter

A drizzle of sweet sherry over winter citrus fruit makes a refreshing addition to a dessert buffet or brunch table.

PREP: 25 MINUTES MAKES 10 FIRST-COURSE SERVINGS

2 pounds navel oranges (about 3 large)

2 1/2 pounds ruby red grapefruits (about 2 large)

1/4 cup fresh cranberries or 1/4 cup pomegranate seeds

2 tablespoons cream sherry

2 tablespoons sugar

fresh kumquats with leaves

1. With knife, cut off slice from tops and bottoms of oranges and grapefruits to steady them. Stand fruit upright on board and slice off peel and white pith, turning fruit as you cut. Repeat with remaining fruit. Slice fruit crosswise into 1/4-inch-thick rounds; cut grapefruit slices in half if large. Place fruit in deep platter, overlapping slices slightly.

2. Sprinkle fruit with cranberries. In cup, stir sherry and sugar until sugar dissolves. Spoon sherry mixture over fruit. Cover and refrigerate up to 1 day if not serving right away. Garnish with kumquats.

Each serving: About 55 calories, 1g protein, 14g carbohydrate, 0g total fat, 2g fiber, 0mg cholesterol, 1mg sodium.

Holiday Citrus Platter

Raspberry-Walnut Streusel Bars

An easy and delicious treat: raspberry jam sandwiched between a buttery cookie bottom and a crumbly streusel top.

PREP: 30 MINUTES   BAKE: 45 MINUTES   MAKES 24 BARS

3/4 cup butter or margarine (1 1/2 sticks), softened
1 cup sugar
1/2 teaspoon freshly grated lemon peel
1/2 teaspoon ground cinnamon
2 large egg yolks

1 teaspoon vanilla extract
2 cups all-purpose flour
1/4 teaspoon salt
1 cup walnuts (4 ounces), toasted and chopped
1/2 cup seedless raspberry jam

1. Preheat oven to 350°F. Evenly grease 9-inch square baking pan.

2. In large bowl, with mixer at medium speed, beat butter, sugar, lemon peel, and cinnamon until light and fluffy, occasionally scraping bowl with rubber spatula. Reduce speed to low; beat in egg yolks and vanilla until well combined, frequently scraping bowl. Add flour and salt and beat just until blended, occasionally scraping bowl. With wooden spoon, stir in walnuts (mixture will be crumbly).

3. With lightly floured hand, pat half of dough evenly onto bottom of prepared pan. Spread raspberry jam over dough, leaving 1/4-inch border all around. With lightly floured hands, pinch off 1-inch pieces of remaining dough and drop randomly on top of jam (it's okay if dough pieces touch); do not pat.

4. Bake until golden, 45 to 50 minutes. Cool completely in pan on wire rack.

5. When cool, cut into 4 strips, then cut each strip crosswise into 6 pieces.

Each bar: About 176 calories, 2g protein, 22g carbohydrate, 10g total fat (4g saturated), 1g fiber, 33mg cholesterol, 86mg sodium.

Brandy Snaps

These lacy cookies are a welcome addition to any homemade cookie assortment. Make them in dry weather or they will be sticky.

PREP: 25 MINUTES BAKE: 5 MINUTES PER BATCH
MAKES ABOUT 24 COOKIES

1/2 cup butter (1 stick, do not use margarine)
3 tablespoons light (mild) molasses
1/2 cup all-purpose flour

1/2 cup sugar
1 teaspoon ground ginger
1/4 teaspoon salt
2 tablespoons brandy

1. Preheat oven to 350°F. Grease large cookie sheet.
2. In 2-quart saucepan, melt butter with molasses over medium-low heat, stirring occasionally, until smooth. Remove from heat. With wooden spoon, stir in flour, sugar, ginger, and salt until blended and smooth; stir in brandy. Set saucepan in bowl of hot water to keep warm.
3. Drop 1 teaspoon batter on prepared cookie sheet; with small metal spatula, spread in circular motion to make 4-inch round (during baking, batter will spread and fill in any thin areas). Repeat to make 4 rounds in all, placing them 2 inches apart. (Do not place more than 4 cookies on sheet.)
4. Bake until golden brown, about 5 minutes. Cool 30 to 60 seconds on cookie sheet on wire rack, just until edges have set; with wide spatula, quickly flip cookies.
5. Working as quickly as possible, roll up each cookie around handle (1/2-inch diameter) of wooden spoon or dowel. If cookies become too hard to roll, briefly return to oven to soften. As each cookie is shaped, slip off spoon handle and cool completely on wire racks.
6. Repeat with remaining batter.

Each cookie: About 72 calories, 0g protein, 8g carbohydrate, 4g total fat (2g saturated), 0g fiber, 10mg cholesterol, 64mg sodium.

Pecan Tassies

Tender pat-in-the-pan crust makes these bite size pies a cinch to prepare.

PREP: 40 MINUTES PLUS CHILLING   BAKE: 30 MINUTES
MAKES 24 COOKIES

1 package (3 ounces) cream cheese, softened
1/2 cup butter or margarine (1 stick), softened, plus 1 tablespoon, melted
1 cup all-purpose flour
2 tablespoons granulated sugar
1 cup pecans (4 ounces), toasted and finely chopped
2/3 cup packed brown sugar
1 large egg
1 teaspoon vanilla extract

1. Preheat oven to 350°F. In large bowl, with mixer at high speed, beat cream cheese and 1/2 cup butter until creamy. Reduce speed to low; add flour and granulated sugar and beat until well combined. Cover and refrigerate 30 minutes.

2. In medium bowl, with wooden spoon, mix pecans, brown sugar, egg, 1 tablespoon melted butter, and vanilla.

3. With floured hands, divide chilled dough into 24 equal pieces (dough will be very soft). With floured fingertips, gently press each piece of dough evenly onto bottom and up sides of ungreased 1 3/4-inch by 1-inch miniature muffin-pan cups. Spoon heaping teaspoon pecan filling into each pastry cup.

4. Bake until filling has set and crust is golden, about 30 minutes. With small knife, loosen cookie cups from muffin-pan cups; transfer to wire racks to cool.

Each cookie: About 131 calories, 1g protein, 12g carbohydrate, 9g total fat (4g saturated), 1g fiber, 24mg cholesterol, 60mg sodium.

Good Housekeeping's Fudgy Brownies

These brownies are fabulous with or without the pecan topping.

PREP: 10 MINUTES   BAKE: 30 MINUTES   MAKES 24 BROWNIES

3/4 cup butter or margarine (1 1/2 sticks)
4 squares (4 ounces) unsweetened chocolate, chopped
4 squares (4 ounces) semisweet chocolate, chopped

2 cups sugar
1 tablespoon vanilla extract
5 large eggs, beaten
1 1/4 cups all-purpose flour
1/2 teaspoon salt

1. Preheat oven to 350°F. Grease 13" by 9" baking pan.
2. In 4-quart saucepan, melt butter and chocolates over low heat, stirring, until smooth. Remove from heat. With wooden spoon, stir in sugar and vanilla. Add eggs; stir until well mixed. Stir flour and salt into chocolate mixture just until blended. Spread batter evenly in prepared pan.
3. Bake until toothpick inserted 1 inch from edge comes out clean, about 30 minutes. Cool completely in pan on wire rack; Cut into 24 pieces.

Each brownie: About 206 calories, 3g protein, 26g carbohydrate, 11g total fat (6g saturated), 1g fiber, 60mg cholesterol, 121mg sodium.

Praline-Iced Brownies

Prepare brownies as directed; cool. In 2-quart saucepan, heat **5 table-spoons butter or margarine** and **1/3 cup packed brown sugar** over medium-low heat until mixture has melted and bubbles, about 5 minutes. Remove from heat. With wire whisk, beat in **3 tablespoons bourbon** or **1 tablespoon vanilla extract** plus **2 tablespoons water**; stir in **2 cups confectioners' sugar** until smooth. With small metal spatula, spread topping over room-temperature brownies; sprinkle 1/2 **cup pecans,** toasted and coarsely chopped, over topping. Cut into 64 pieces.

Each brownie: About 297 calories, 3g protein, 39g carbohydrate, 15g total fat (8g saturated), 2g fiber, 66mg cholesterol, 147mg sodium.

Lemon Bars

If you like, prepare lemon bars up to a day ahead: Prepare through step 4, but do not top with sugar. Refrigerate until ready to serve. Sprinkle with confectioners' sugar before cutting into bars.

PREP: 25 MINUTES PLUS COOLING   BAKE: ABOUT 38 MINUTES
MAKES 32 LEMON BARS

3/4 cup butter (1 1/2 sticks), softened
   (no substitutions)
2 1/4 cups all-purpose flour
2/3 cup plus 1 tablespoon
   confectioners' sugar

3 to 4 large lemons
6 large eggs
2 cups granulated sugar
1 teaspoon baking powder
3/4 teaspoon salt

1. Preheat oven to 350°F. Grease 13" by 9" metal baking pan. Line pan with foil, extending foil over rim; lightly grease foil. (Or, line pan with nonstick foil, but do not grease.)

2. In food processor with knife blade attached, pulse butter, 2 cups flour, and 2/3 cup confectioners' sugar until mixture is moist but crumbly. Dough should hold together when pressed between 2 fingers. Sprinkle mixture evenly into prepared pan. With fingertips, press dough onto bottom of pan. Bake until lightly browned, 20 to 25 minutes.

3. While crust bakes, prepare filling: From lemons, grate 2 1/2 teaspoons peel and squeeze 2/3 cup juice. In large bowl, with wire whisk, beat eggs. Add lemon peel and juice, granulated sugar, baking powder, salt, and remaining 1/4 cup flour; whisk until well blended.

4. Whisk filling again and pour onto hot crust. Bake until filling is just set and golden around edges, 18 to 22 minutes. Transfer pan to wire rack. Sift remaining 1 tablespoon confectioners' sugar over warm filling. Cool completely in pan on wire rack.

5. When cool, transfer with foil to cutting board. Carefully pull foil from sides of lemon bar. If you like, trim edges. Cut lengthwise into 4 strips, then cut each strip crosswise into 8 pieces.

Each lemon bar: About 145 calories, 2g protein, 23g carbohydrate, 5g total fat (3g saturated), 1g fiber, 52mg cholesterol, 55mg sodium.

INDEX

METRIC CONVERSION CHARTS

The recipes that appear in this cookbook use the standard United States method for measuring liquid and dry or solid ingredients (teaspoons, tablespoons, and cups). The information on this chart is provided to help cooks outside the U.S. successfully use these recipes. All equivalents are approximate.

METRIC EQUIVALENTS FOR DIFFERENT TYPES OF INGREDIENTS

A standard cup measure of a dry or solid ingredient will vary in weight depending on the type of ingredient. A standard cup of liquid is the same volume for any type of liquid. Use the following chart when converting standard cup measures to grams (weight) or milliliters (volume).

Standard Cup	Fine Powder (e.g. flour)	Grain (e.g. rice)	Granular (e.g. sugar)	Liquid Solids (e.g. butter)	Liquid (e.g. milk)
1	140 g	150 g	190 g	200 g	240 ml
$3/4$	105 g	113 g	143 g	150 g	180 ml
$2/3$	93 g	100 g	125 g	133 g	160 ml
$1/2$	70 g	75 g	95 g	100 g	120 ml
$1/3$	47 g	50 g	63 g	67 g	80 ml
$1/4$	35 g	38 g	48 g	50 g	60 ml
$1/8$	18 g	19 g	24 g	25 g	30 ml

USEFUL EQUIVALENTS FOR LIQUID INGREDIENTS BY VOLUME

$1/4$ tsp	=				1 ml
$1/2$ tsp	=				2 ml
1 tsp	=				5 ml
3 tsp	=	1 tbls	=	$1/2$ fl oz =	15 ml
		2 tbls	=	$1/8$ cup =	1 fl oz = 30 ml
		4 tbls	=	$1/4$ cup =	2 fl oz = 60 ml
		$5^1/3$ tbls	=	$1/3$ cup =	3 fl oz = 80 ml
		8 tbls	=	$1/2$ cup =	4 fl oz = 120 ml
		$10^2/3$ tbls	=	$2/3$ cup =	5 fl oz = 160 ml
		12 tbls	=	$3/4$ cup =	6 fl oz = 180 ml
		16 tbls	=	1 cup =	8 fl oz = 240 ml
		1 pt	=	2 cups =	16 fl oz = 480 ml
		1 qt	=	4 cups =	32 fl oz = 960 ml
					33 fl oz = 1000 ml = 1l

USEFUL EQUIVALENTS FOR DRY INGREDIENTS BY WEIGHT

(To convert ounces to grams, multiply the number of ounces by 30.)

1 oz	=	$1/16$ lb	=	30 g
4 oz	=	$1/4$ lb	=	120 g
8 oz	=	$1/2$ lb	=	240 g
12 oz	=	$3/4$ lb	=	360 g
16 oz	=	1 lb	=	480 g

USEFUL EQUIVALENTS FOR COOKING/OVEN TEMPERATURES

	Fahrenheit	Celsius	Gas Mark
Freeze Water	32° F	0° C	
Room Temperature	68° F	20° C	
Boil Water	212° F	100° C	
Bake	325° F	160° C	3
	350° F	180° C	4
	375° F	190° C	5
	400° F	200° C	6
	425° F	220° C	7
	450° F	230° C	8
Broil			Grill

USEFUL EQUIVALENTS FOR LENGTH

(To convert inches to centimeters, multiply the number of inches by 2.5.)

1 in	=		2.5 cm
6 in	=	$1/2$ ft =	15 cm
12 in	=	1 ft =	30 cm
36 in	=	3 ft = 1 yd =	90 cm
40 in	=		100 cm = 1 m